FLORENCE TRAVEL GU 2024

How To Spend A Day In Florence Without Breaking The Bank, And Walk And Explore The Historic Center In Italy!

GEORGIA TUCKER

Georgia Tucker

COPYRIGHT

No part of this book may be reproduced in any written, electronic, recording, or photocopying without written permission of the publisher or author.

The exception would be in the case of brief quotations embodied in the critical articles or reviews and pages where permission is specifically granted by the publisher or author.

Although every precaution has been taken to verify the accuracy of the information contained herein, the author and publisher assume no responsibility for any errors or omissions. No liability is assumed for damages that may result from the use of the information contained within.

All Right Reserved©2023

Georgia Tucker

TABLE OF CONTENTS

TABLE OF CONTENTS	2
INTRODUCTION	9
WELCOME TO FLORENCE	9
WHY VISIT FLORENCE	11
CHAPTER ONE	23
BRIEF HISTORY OF FLORENCE	23
PLANNING YOUR TRIP/ FLORENCE ESSENTIALS	25
BEST TIME TO VISIT FLORENCE	26
FLORENCE WEATHER BY MONTH	28
CHAPTER TWO	31
FLORENCE TRAVEL TIPS 101	31
FAVORITE THINGS TO DO IN FLORENCE (AND HOW TO DO THEM!)	37
CHAPTER THREE	59
GREAT ITINERARIES, 1,2,3 DAYS	59
CHAPTER FOUR	105
BEST LOCAL DISHES AND DRINKS FROM FLORENCE	105

THE BEST RESTAURANTS IN FLORENCE	114

CHAPTER FIVE — 129

TOP-RATED TOURIST ATTRACTIONS IN FLORENCE, ITALY	129

CHAPTER SIX — 147

21 BEST MUSEUMS IN FLORENCE	147
TIPS FOR VISITING THE MUSEUMS IN FLORENCE	179
THE 15 BEST BEACHES NEAR FLORENCE, ITALY (2023)	181

CHAPTER SEVEN — 193

WHERE TO GO SHOPPING IN FLORENCE	193
I LOVE SHOPPING IN FLORENCE!	198
A COMPLETE GUIDE TO SHOPPING FOR LEATHER IN FLORENCE	203
SHOPPING TIPS	211
A SHOE-BUYING GUIDE IN FLORENCE	215

CHAPTER EIGHT — 219

THE BEST HOTELS IN FLORENCE	219
HOW WE CHOOSE THE BEST HOTELS IN FLORENCE (TIPS)	219

CHAPTER NINE — 233

HEALTH AND SAFETY IN FLORENCE	233
MONEY SAVING TIPS	235

CHAPTER TEN — 241

GETTING AROUND FLORENCE — 241
HOW TO MAKE THE MOST OUT OF YOUR TRIP TO FLORENCE — 246

CONCLUSION — 249

Georgia Tucker

Georgia Tucker

Georgia Tucker

INTRODUCTION

WELCOME TO FLORENCE

Welcome to " Florence Travel Guide 2023-2024: How to Spend a Day in Florence Without Breaking the Bank and Walk and Explore the Historic Center in Italy!" This comprehensive travel guide is designed to help you discover all that this stunning city has to offer without overspending.

Florence is a city that has captured the hearts of travelers for centuries. Founded in 59 BC, Florence has a rich history that is reflected in its stunning architecture, art, and culture. From the Renaissance era to the modern day, Florence has been a hub of creativity, innovation, and inspiration. The city is known for its incredible art collections, including works by famous artists such as Michelangelo, Leonardo da Vinci, and Botticelli. It's also famous for its beautiful architecture, with iconic landmarks such as the Duomo, Ponte Vecchio, and Uffizi Gallery.

However, with so many attractions and experiences to enjoy, it can be easy to overspend. That's where this guide comes in. We've done the research and put together a detailed plan for exploring Florence that won't break the bank.

In this guide, we'll take you through the most iconic landmarks of Florence, starting with the Duomo. This stunning cathedral is a must-see attraction, and our guide will show you how to visit without spending a fortune. We'll also provide insider tips for getting the best views, avoiding the crowds, and experiencing the cathedral to its fullest.

Next up is the Ponte Vecchio, the oldest bridge in Florence. This iconic landmark is famous for its jewelry shops and stunning views of the Arno River. Our guide will show you how to visit the bridge without breaking the bank, including how to find affordable souvenirs and take the best photos. The Uffizi Gallery is another must-see attraction in Florence, with one of the world's most impressive art collections. Our guide will show you how to visit the gallery for free, including how to book tickets in advance and which days are free to visit. We'll also provide insider tips for getting the most out of your visit and avoiding the crowds.

Of course, no trip to Florence would be complete without indulging in its delicious cuisine. We'll show you how to savor the flavors of traditional Tuscan cuisine without breaking the bank. From street food to local markets, we'll introduce you to the best affordable food options in the city, so you can indulge in Italian delicacies without overspending.

Finally, we'll show you how to explore the charming streets and hidden corners of the historic center on foot. With our walking tour recommendations, you'll discover the most beautiful and fascinating spots in Florence while taking in all the sights and sounds of this vibrant city. We'll also provide tips for navigating the city's public transportation system, so you can easily get around without spending a fortune.

Whether you're a first-time visitor or a seasoned traveler, this guide will help you experience Florence in all its glory without overspending. Join us on a journey through one of the most beautiful cities in the world and discover why Florence is a must-visit destination for any traveler.

WHY VISIT FLORENCE

In 1904, Mark Twain characterized Florence as a city that evokes dreams, reflecting the sentiments expressed by numerous individuals about this remarkable destination. Despite its status as a popular tourist hotspot, Florence retains a captivating blend of small-town charm and vibrant urban energy.

Georgia Tucker

With its enchanting vistas at every turn, superb dining establishments offering delectable Italian cuisine, and picturesque cobblestone streets that invite the embrace of Dolce Far Niente (the pleasure of doing nothing), Florence stands as one of the foremost locations for immersing oneself in the quintessential Italian atmosphere.

Birthplace Of Italian Language

During the late 18th century, the Tuscan dialect was adopted as the official language of Italy, owing to its prominence in Florence. It is believed that Dante, a native of Florence and a renowned poet, composed his verses in the Florentine dialect, thereby elevating both himself and the dialect to nationwide recognition. Consequently, Florentine dialect emerged as the most widely acknowledged variant throughout Italy. If you possess an interest in language acquisition, including Florence in your itinerary allows for an opportunity to explore the local before your journey.

Filled With Culture

Regarded as one of Italy's and indeed the world's most culturally rich cities, Florence's historic center has held the distinction of being a UNESCO World Heritage site since 1982. Flourishing from its central location, influential inhabitants, and prosperous merchants, Florence played a pivotal role in fostering Europe's most prosperous period of cultural achievements, evident in its art, architecture, and even culinary traditions.

Florence Is A Walkable City

The pinnacle of our recommendations concerning why Florence should be a prime consideration for your next visit to Italy awaits. The entire Renaissance-era old town is conveniently traversable on foot. Year after year, millions of tourists delight in wandering the narrow thoroughfares of Florence, as the city restricts vehicular traffic on its momentous cobblestone lanes to enhance accessibility. Embarking on a leisurely exploration of Florence's old town streets proves to be an exquisite experience, thereby solidifying its reputation as one of the world's preeminent walkable urban centers.

Within approximately two hours, one can independently traverse the principal landmarks. Alternatively, we suggest partaking in a complimentary walking tour of Florence, which offers insights into renowned locales. Secure your reservation for a free walking tour of Florence today. Rest assured, it is entirely feasible to traverse the entirety of the old town within a mere half-hour, including a passage across both banks of the Arno River, taking in the breathtaking view from the iconic Ponte Vecchio.

Most Famous Galleries In The World | Uffizi Gallery

Florence is synonymous with art, particularly the masterpieces of the Renaissance. The city houses one of the world's most illustrious art museums, the Uffizi Gallery, where an abundance of works by esteemed Italian artists such as Giotto, Botticelli, and Michelangelo are showcased.

This world-class gallery, designed by the celebrated artist and architect Giorgio Vasari, was constructed over a span of 20 years, from 1560 to 1580, and now occupies the first and second floors

Georgia Tucker

of a grand edifice situated along the riverbanks. Within its chambers lie treasured monuments, sculptures, and paintings dating back to the Middle Ages and beyond. A visit to the Uffizi Gallery is an essential undertaking when exploring the city, and due to the perpetually long queues, we recommend securing skip-the-line tickets in advance. The view from the Ponte Vecchio is nothing short of stunning, solidifying its status as one of Florence's most captivating spots, perfect for capturing memorable photographs to share on social media.

Incredible Photo Spots

As evidenced by our blog, we possess a fervent passion for picturesque locations, collecting postcards from the places we visit. Leaving our mark on each destination catalyzes cherishing memories and sparking conversations with our acquaintances.

Among the many reasons to visit Florence, the abundance of incredible photo spots ranks highly. From the hilltop perch of Piazzale Michelangelo, one can survey the entire city sprawling below. Whether during the early morning when few others are present or throughout the day, one can capture exquisite images of the Ponte Vecchio, either from a nearby bridge with the river flowing beneath or while strolling along the storied cobblestone streets steeped in history and legend.

Unique Hidden Gems In Florence

Echoing our previous sentiments, we relish the experience of losing ourselves in exploration. Florence facilitates this endeavor with its easy navigability, allowing us to meander through its narrow streets at a leisurely pace. Uncover the city's hidden gems or simply spend time idling along the riverside, seeking out the most picturesque vantage points for witnessing the splendid sunset.

We recommend adopting a relaxed approach when immersing yourself in Florence, embracing the local lifestyle. Indulge in an aperitif at a neighborhood bar or savor the delights of the city's outdoor spaces. Among Florence's lesser-known treasures, don't miss Via Toscanella for an enthralling display of local street art. For an authentic experience, visit Piazza Ciompi, where you'll find the renowned Florence Flea Market, featuring a treasure trove of second-hand items and antique decorations.

Venture into Palazzo Vecchio, which offers free admission, and serves as the seat of the local council. As you enter Palazzo Vecchio, you'll be captivated by the sculpture "Perseus with the head of Medusa" by Benvenuto Cellini. Finally, don't overlook the Boboli Gardens, an enchanting hidden oasis in Florence that warrants a visit, particularly during the vibrant season of spring.

Open-air Museum

Renowned for its abundance of art and culture, Florence stands as an open-air museum that captivates visitors at every turn. With a simple step out of your hotel, you are greeted with a wealth of historical wonders, exquisite exhibits, and stunning architecture, requiring no elaborate itinerary.

For an enriching experience without spending a penny, we recommend exploring Piazza della Signoria, a square brimming with magnificent buildings, statues, and fountains. To avoid crowds, consider an early morning visit, as we did in June, when the Loggia dei Lanzi can be fully appreciated, along with the

Georgia Tucker

iconic Palazzo Vecchio, the 16th-century Fountain of Neptune, and the David statue at the entrance of the council palace.

To make the most of your visit, we suggest booking a free walking tour of Florence in the morning and reserving a visit to the Salone dei Cinquecento (Hall of the five hundred).

Creativity Everywhere (Street Artists)
Florence has long been a gathering place for both local and international street artists eager to showcase their talents throughout the city. Sottopasso delle Cure stands as one of the prime locations to admire the vibrant street art scene.

Delicious Food In Florence
For food enthusiasts and those with adventurous palates, Florence's cuisine offers a captivating blend of culture and flavors that will leave you astounded. The local Florentine food incorporates the freshest ingredients sourced from the Tuscan region. Make sure to try "Schiaccia," a delectable focaccia-panini filled with regional ingredients. While Antico Vinaio is a renowned establishment, we encourage you to seek out local gems such as "La Cantinetta" and "Lo Schiacciavino." Share your experiences with us in the comments!

Explore Florence's Local Markets
Wandering through the bustling markets of Florence is a must-do experience, whether you're searching for the perfect souvenir, sampling Tuscan produce, or simply immersing yourself in the lively atmosphere. While the famous "San Lorenzo Outdoor

Market" offers a bazaar-like experience and showcases local products, it's essential to exercise caution and differentiate between genuine and counterfeit items. To embrace a more authentic local vibe, consider visiting the Florence Central Market in the San Lorenzo neighborhood. This 19th-century indoor market hall provides an array of culinary delights. Additionally, don't miss the Mercato Nuovo, also known as Mercato Porcellino, known for its proximity to famous sightseeing spots. This market primarily offers leather products, jackets, bags, and belts.

Learn How To Make Pasta In Florence

To immerse yourself in an authentic Italian experience, we highly recommend booking a pasta-making class in Florence. This exciting activity unveils the secrets of preparing delicious and original Tuscan meals. Your journey begins with a visit to the local market, where a skilled chef will guide you in selecting the finest fresh ingredients. Indulge in a top-notch culinary lesson, mastering the art of pasta-making, and impress your guests back home with authentic Italian dishes. Discover the superb cooking classes available in Florence.

Sip Wine On The Hills

Nestled within the renowned Chianti region, Florence provides an excellent opportunity to indulge in the best-value yet delectable varieties of wine directly from the source. Numerous wine-tasting tours offer a chance to explore authentic Italian wineries and vineyards. Take a day trip from Florence to Chianti, where you can not only sample wines but also admire the picturesque ancient villages, breathtaking scenery, and olive groves.

Georgia Tucker

Fashion Streets

Florence stands as a mecca for fashion enthusiasts seeking to add Italy's renowned craftsmanship and leather goods to their collections. Via de' Tornabuoni, Via del Parione, Via dei Calzaiuoli, and Mercato di San Lorenzo rank among the best shopping streets in Florence. Like many other Italian cities, Florence exudes style, and I have had the privilege of exploring the city on numerous occasions, attending the annual fashion show held at Palazzo Pitti. So, whether you pack your best dresses for the trip or look forward to shopping in Italy, Florence won't disappoint.

Romantic City

With its charming architectural designs spanning centuries and an enchanting Italian ambiance, Florence stands among the most romantic cities in the world. Whether you take a stroll through the Bardini gardens, particularly captivating in spring with the presence of Listeria passages, or witness a mesmerizing sunset along the banks of the River Arno, this city is an idyllic destination for lovebirds. For more romantic city recommendations in Italy, consult our guide.

Ideal Europe Getaway

Florence beckons as Europe's jewel, where every street, alley, and building resembles a living museum, brimming with history. This Tuscan city not only offers some of the world's finest hotels but also serves as a hub for art, delectable cuisine, and captivating culture. Its central location on the peninsula makes it an ideal destination for a vacation in Italy. Whether you choose to explore

Georgia Tucker

Florence exclusively or include it as part of a remarkable road trip that encompasses other incredible towns such as Rome, Milan, Bologna, or Cinque Terre, your European getaway will be truly unforgettable.

CHAPTER ONE

BRIEF HISTORY OF FLORENCE

Florence is a city located in central Italy and serves as the capital of the Tuscany region. The city has a long and complex history that spans back to the Roman era, but it is most famously known for being the birthplace of the Italian Renaissance during the 14th century.

During the medieval period, Florence established itself as a significant center for trade and banking. This economic power allowed the city to become an important city-state within Italy. The wealth that the city gained during this time also provided a foundation for Florence to become a hub for the arts. Many influential artists and writers, including Giotto, Boccaccio, and Dante Alighieri, called Florence home.

The 14th century brought an exciting period of growth and development to Florence. The city became the epicenter of a cultural and intellectual revolution known as the Renaissance. This era saw the emergence of incredible artistic talent, including the likes of Leonardo da Vinci, Michelangelo, and Sandro Botticelli, who are widely regarded as some of the greatest artists of all time. Alongside the visual arts, Florence became a center of literature, philosophy, and science. Prominent thinkers, such as Galileo Galilei and Niccolo Machiavelli, made their mark on the city.

However, this period of growth was not without its challenges. Political power struggles and conflicts were a common occurrence in Florence, with powerful families like the Medici family rising to prominence. Despite their patronage of the arts, these powerful families also used their influence to maintain political control, leading to periods of instability and upheaval.

Despite these difficulties, Florence continued to flourish as a center for the arts, culture, and commerce in the centuries that followed. Today, it is a popular tourist destination that attracts visitors from around the world. The city is renowned for its beautiful architecture, museums, and art galleries, which showcase the legacy of Florence's rich cultural history.

Florence Today

Today, Florence is a bustling and vibrant city that continues to be a center for art, culture, and commerce. The city is home to many famous landmarks, such as the Ponte Vecchio, the Uffizi Gallery, and the Cathedral of Santa Maria del Fiore.

Tourism is a significant part of Florence's economy, with millions of visitors coming to the city each year. Visitors are drawn to the city's many art galleries and museums, which house some of the world's most renowned art collections, including works by Michelangelo, Leonardo da Vinci, and Botticelli. The city's beautiful architecture, charming narrow streets, and picturesque squares also make it a popular destination for tourists.

In addition to its rich cultural heritage, Florence is also a center for commerce and industry. The city is home to many small and medium-sized enterprises, particularly in the fashion and design industries. The city is known for its high-quality leather goods, clothing, and jewelry, and many international brands have their headquarters in Florence.

Florence is also a center for education and research, with several universities and research centers located in the city. The University of Florence is one of the oldest and most prestigious universities in Italy and is well-regarded for its humanities and social sciences programs.

Overall, Florence is a city that continues to thrive as a center for art, culture, commerce, and education, and it remains an important destination for visitors from all over the world.

PLANNING YOUR TRIP/ FLORENCE ESSENTIALS

Where Is Florence?
Florence is situated in Tuscany, a central region of the Italian Peninsula. Its strategic positioning historically made it a crucial gateway between the South and North of Italy. Being approximately 145 miles away from Rome and just a one-hour train ride from Milan, Florence was once the capital of Italy. The city is surrounded by captivating landscapes, featuring gently rolling hills that offer breathtaking views of the country. From Florence, you can conveniently access the picturesque Cinque Terre or immerse yourself in the countryside villas of Tuscany.

Georgia Tucker

BEST TIME TO VISIT FLORENCE

Planning a visit to Florence can be challenging due to its popularity, but you can still enjoy pleasant weather while avoiding the crowds. The best times to visit Florence are March to April or September to October when the number of tourists is generally lower, and the weather remains favorable. The peak tourist season in Florence spans from late June to the end of August, during which prices skyrocket. Although the city can be crowded during this time, the experience is still worthwhile.

How To Get To Florence

Florence has its international airport known as "Peretola" or Amerigo Vespucci Airport. Additionally, Pisa Airport, located approximately 43 miles from the city center, offers convenient access to Florence. Other feasible options include Bologna, Perugia, Genoa, Rome, and Milan, especially for visitors from Canada or the US. From the airport, you can reach Florence by shuttle bus, taxi, or train, depending on the chosen airport. To navigate within Florence, obtaining a city card that includes transportation and discounts on select attractions is highly recommended. The city is conveniently located along the A1 Autostrade, the main Italian motorway connecting Naples to Milan. Moreover, Florence serves as a major hub for high-speed trains, enabling easy rail travel from various cities across Italy, including Milan and Rome. The primary railway station, Santa Maria Novella, is conveniently situated near the city center.

When Visit Florence

As Italians, we have explored Florence on multiple occasions and during different periods. While the city is always charming to discover, the number of tourists is a crucial factor to consider. April, May, September, and October are particularly favorable due to a balanced influx of tourists and pleasant weather. Spring in Italy is truly enchanting. However, if you prefer the vibrant atmosphere of summer, Florence from May to September offers warm sun, delightful outdoor spaces, art festivals, and galleries. Nevertheless, bear in mind that this period tends to be crowded. For fewer tourists and better accommodation deals, consider visiting Florence during the winter months. January, being the coldest month in Tuscany with unfavorable weather conditions, is best avoided.

What Is Florence Famous For?

Located in the heart of the Tuscan region, Florence has a rich history that dates back to its origins as a Roman city and its subsequent development into a flourishing medieval community. Today, it has evolved into a prominent tourist destination, renowned for its historical and cultural significance worldwide. In addition to housing iconic landmarks like the Ponte Vecchio, Florence is celebrated for its natural beauty and architectural marvels. If you're still contemplating why Florence should be on your itinerary, explore the following unique activities and attractions that define this remarkable city.

Georgia Tucker

FLORENCE WEATHER BY MONTH

Spring (April To June) And Autumn (September To October)

As Italians, we have had the opportunity to visit Florence on multiple occasions and during various periods. While the city is always delightful to explore, the number of tourists present tends to vary from one month to another. Bearing this in mind, it is advisable to consider visiting Florence in April, May, September, or October, as these months strike a favorable balance between tourist numbers and pleasant weather. The beauty of spring in Italy is particularly enchanting, as exemplified in our guide. However, if you prefer the vibrant atmosphere of summer, the period from May to September offers ample sunshine, welcoming outdoor spaces, art festivals, and galleries. It is important to note, however, that this period is characterized by heightened crowds. For those seeking fewer tourists and attractive accommodation deals, exploring Florence during the winter months is recommended. It is advisable to avoid visiting in January, which is the coldest month in Tuscany, known for its inclement weather conditions of rain and wind.

25 Things To Do In Florence

- Cattedrale di Santa Maria del Fiore (Florence Cathedral)
- Uffizi Gallery
- Galleria dell'Accademia (Original David of Donatello)
- Florence Central Market (Mercato Centrale)
- Palazzo Vecchio (Hall of Five Hundreds)

- Piazza della Signoria
- Fiesole Hill
- Lungarno (Arno River Banks)
- Boboli Gardens
- Giotto Bell Tower
- Brunelleschi Dome
- Piazzale Michelangelo
- Giardino Bardini
- Santo Spirito Market
- Ponte Vecchio
- Basilica di Santa Croce
- Baptistery of St. John
- Basilica di San Lorenzo
- Strozzi's Palace
- Piazza della Signoria
- Palazzo Pitti
- Church of Santa Maria Novella
- Church of San Miniato al Monte (Hidden gems of Florence)
- Vasari Corridor
- Hog statue

Georgia Tucker

How Many Days In Florence?

Our extensive exploration of Florence has consistently revealed new hidden gems within the city, making each visit a beautiful and enriching experience. While there is no fixed duration required to fully appreciate Florence, we have curated a collection of exceptional guides to assist you in planning your trip. Allotting two days to explore the city will enable you to visit its most significant landmarks, although it may not allow ample time to fully appreciate the outdoor spaces. During our initial visit to Florence in the summer, we discovered that an early start was necessary to enjoy the city's charm without the presence of large crowds. However, if you choose to visit in winter, this becomes relatively easier, and a one-day stay in the city might be sufficient. For detailed recommendations on exploring Florence within a day, we encourage you to consult our dedicated guide.

CHAPTER TWO

FLORENCE TRAVEL TIPS 101

Below, we present a valuable assortment of tips and insights to enhance your Florence experience. Take note and appreciate the difference they can make!

#1 Watch out For Streetside Art

While visiting renowned museums and galleries such as the Uffizi and Accademia is highly recommended, do not overlook the artistic wonders that adorn the streets of Florence. The city itself is a masterpiece, and you will encounter captivating street art on various corners. Exploring gardens, squares, churches, and fountains will introduce you to remarkable and familiar artistic expressions.

#2 Always Carry Cash!

In the Tuscan region, ATMs often impose high fees for transactions made with Visa and Mastercard. Whenever possible, consider bringing an ample supply of Euros from your home country to avoid these commission charges. Additionally, tipping is customary in Florence, so having spare change on hand is practical.

#3 Spot The Right Gelato

Gelato holds a cherished place in Italian cuisine, and if you desire an authentic gelato experience characterized by its rich and fruity flavors, steer clear of shops that showcase vibrant, towering displays of gelato. A true gelato masterpiece exhibits a soft texture that melts in your mouth, free from preservatives. Look for gelato served from refrigerated tubs and featuring pale colors reminiscent of the fruit used in its preparation. For guidance on the best gelato shops in Florence, consult reliable sources.

#4 Pre-Book Your Skip The Line Tickets Online

Florence boasts numerous galleries and museums housing some of the world's most iconic artworks and sculptures. Consequently, these attractions can become incredibly crowded, particularly during the summer season, often resulting in long waiting times of up to two hours. To circumvent this inconvenience, we recommend securing skip-the-line tickets online well in advance. By doing so, you can save yourself from enduring the scorching Tuscan sun and enjoy additional discounts on your tickets.

#5 Be Vigilant About Your Belongings
Florence has unfortunately witnessed a high occurrence of petty crimes, with purse snatching and pickpocketing being the most prevalent. Safeguard your belongings by carrying a small pouch attached to your belt and discreetly hidden beneath your clothing to protect your passports, cash, and ATM cards. Exercise particular caution when navigating crowded tourist areas like the Florence Duomo and Uffizi Gallery, both indoors and while waiting in queues.

#6 Get Out Of The Historic Center
For a more enchanting and idyllic Florence, venture beyond the bustling areas surrounding Duomo or Palazzo Vecchio. Discover the charm of neighborhoods like Santo Spirito or San Niccolo, where you will encounter quaint bakeries, flower-adorned houses, vibrant gardens, cobblestone streets, and picturesque scenes of colorful mopeds. Unveil hidden surprises such as family-operated art galleries, intimate squares with charming fountains, and olive groves atop hills.

#7 Wi-Fi Spots Abound
Florence embraces its tech-savvy reputation, offering numerous open Wi-Fi networks throughout the city. Italian phone users can enjoy one hour of complimentary internet access in the city center. Many restaurants and cafes also provide Wi-Fi connectivity, making them ideal spots for digital nomads to unwind and work. If you don't spot a Wi-Fi sign, don't hesitate to

inquire with the receptionist or waitstaff for the password, as they will be happy to assist you.

#8 Explore The Tuscan Countryside

Escape the confines of Florence and immerse yourself in the lush heartland of Tuscany, adorned with ancient vineyards and olive groves interspersed among medieval villages. Select from a variety of destinations, including the verdant rolling hills of Chianti, the UNESCO World Heritage sites of San Gimignano, Pisa, and Siena. Embarking on a day trip from Florence grants you a rejuvenating respite from the bustling city squares.

#9 Climb The Duomo Cupola

Though ascending the approximately 500 cramped steps to reach the pinnacle of the Duomo may appear arduous, the breathtaking view awaiting you at the summit is well worth the effort. To secure your place, book your Cupola Climb tickets online well in advance, as they tend to sell out rapidly. Consider undertaking this ascent around dusk, and prepare to witness one of the most awe-inspiring sunsets imaginable.

#10 Watch Out For Stendhal Syndrome!

Remember the adage, "Too much of a good thing"? This adage holds for your visit to Florence as well. Stendhal Syndrome, also known as Florence Syndrome, is a psychosomatic condition characterized by rapid heartbeat, fainting, confusion, and even hallucinations, reportedly triggered by exposure to objects or phenomena of extraordinary beauty. Stay hydrated, explore at a leisurely pace, and indulge your wanderlust sensibly to ensure a delightful and fulfilling experience.

#11 Sign Up For A Food Tour In Florence

Artistry in Florence extends beyond paintings and sculptures to the city's culinary landscape. Engage in a food tour that promises a gastronomic extravaganza, allowing you to savor delectable delights as you leisurely journey from one gastronomic destination to another. Alternatively, visit the Mercado Central, a local food market boasting an artisan food court on the upper level, where you can sample Florence's culinary specialties under one roof.

#12 Catch The Sunrise Over River Arno

Ponte Vecchio, an iconic stone arch bridge spanning the Arno River, is renowned for its jewelry shops housed in small sheds originally designated for butchers. Embrace the early morning tranquility and witness a captivating sunrise from this vantage point. The bridge's vintage backdrop also presents an excellent opportunity for capturing memorable photographs.

#13 Be Street Savvy When It Comes To Shopping

Florence holds the distinction of being Italy's hub for leather goods, offering a tempting array of bags, belts, wallets, and jackets. While many shops are open to negotiation, it is important to note that cash is the preferred payment method.

Additionally, be aware that most shops in Florence observe an afternoon siesta from 1 PM to 4 PM. To enhance your shopping experience, venture beyond the stores near prominent landmarks and explore smaller neighborhood establishments for a wider selection and competitive prices.

#14 Italians Dine Late

In Italy, dinner is typically served after 8:00 PM, and numerous restaurants do not open their doors until 7:30 PM. Before the evening meal, locals often partake in an aperitivo, enjoying a refreshing drink and light snacks at a bar or enoteca (wine bar) during happy hour. If you are accustomed to dining early, consider visiting a neighborhood bar and relish the complimentary snack buffet featuring cured meats and cheeses alongside your cocktail until dinner service commences.

#15 Visit The Lesser Known Boboli Gardens & Pitti Palace

While the Uffizi Gallery, Florence Duomo, and Accademia Gallery attract throngs of tourists, two hidden gems within the city deserve your attention. Enter the expansive 111-acre Boboli Gardens, where terraced gardens, concealed fountains, and enchanting wisteria-covered paths await. Marvel at the 6-meter high obelisk from the time of Ramses II, delighting art and nature enthusiasts alike. Ascend the steep hill within the gardens to reach the pinnacle and be rewarded with breathtaking city views and a sun-soaked lawn, offering respite for weary legs.

Adjacent to the Boboli Gardens lies Palazzo Pitti, an opulent residence once inhabited by grand dukes and monarchs of Florence. Stroll through the Royal Apartments and immerse yourself in the palace's numerous galleries showcasing artistic and historical exhibits. For those seeking a taste of Renaissance art away from the bustling crowds, Palazzo Pitti and Boboli Gardens are an exquisite combination.

FAVORITE THINGS TO DO IN FLORENCE (AND HOW TO DO THEM!)

Without further ado, we present our selection of favorite activities to enjoy in Florence, listed in a rough recommended order. It is important to note that the duration of each activity may vary, with some requiring more time than others (e.g., exploring the Uffizi Gallery versus enjoying a sandwich). Therefore, consider this order as a general guideline. Additionally, we provide comprehensive insights into why each activity is noteworthy, along with practical information such as costs and ticket procurement details. We strive to address the frustrations often experienced when encountering vague recommendations lacking pertinent trip planning details.

Dive Deep Into Renaissance Art In The Uffizi Gallery

The Uffizi Gallery houses a remarkable collection of art, meticulously curated by the Medici family during their reign in Florence. Originally serving as an office building for municipal employees, the structure transformed in the 18th century, becoming a museum of unparalleled significance.

During its early years, access to the Uffizi Gallery was restricted to individuals with exclusive invitations, resembling the select entry system of the Louvre in Paris. Spanning a vast expanse, the gallery's sheer magnitude necessitates ample time to truly appreciate its treasures, as a single day of exploration barely scratches the surface.

However, what sets the Uffizi Gallery apart and secures its prominent position on this list is its exceptional organization. The artworks are thoughtfully arranged in chronological order, allowing visitors to observe the evolution of art in Florence from the pre-Renaissance era through the Enlightenment period, spanning approximately the 14th to 17th centuries.

As you navigate through the Uffizi Gallery, you will encounter masterpieces by renowned Italian artists, including Giotto, heralded by many art historians as the progenitor of modern painting, as well as luminaries such as Leonardo Da Vinci, Michelangelo, Raphael, Donatello (completing the ensemble of the Teenage Mutant Ninja Turtles), and Caravaggio.

Now, let us delve into the logistics of obtaining tickets to the Uffizi Gallery and the benefits of embarking on a guided tour for a more immersive and enriching experience.

Taking A Guided Tour Of The Uffizi For A Richer, Deeper Experience

In all honesty, my inclination toward art museums has never been particularly strong. Typically, after approximately two to three hours, the experience tends to wane, leading to a diminished interest in reading signage and a tendency to mindlessly navigate through the remaining galleries. Consequently, art museums seldom rank high on my list of preferred activities. However, during my recent visit to Italy, I began to comprehend the underlying reasons behind my lukewarm engagement with such institutions.

I struggle to establish a connection with paintings and sculptures when they are presented in isolation. This disconnect arises from my limited knowledge of these art forms, which leaves me uncertain about what aspects to focus on or appreciate. I recall my struggles during high school art classes, the only academic pursuit in which I struggled to perform well. Conversely, when presented with a book—a domain in which I possess significant experience as both a reader and a writer, albeit primarily in non-fiction—I can engage with it on a meaningful level, leveraging my familiarity with the medium and understanding of its nuances.

In Italy, I realized that the presence of a guide—preferably an expert in art history or a related field—can make a world of difference in my museum experience. A guide brings invaluable expertise, providing the contextual background necessary to appreciate the artwork on display. Thus, whenever I explore an art museum, I now ensure that I have a guide or, at the very least, an audio guide to accompany me.

Consequently, my partner and I opted for a guided tour of the Uffizi Gallery in Florence, a decision that we did not regret. Admittedly, the beginning of our tour was somewhat tumultuous, marked by somewhat inhospitable staff and technical difficulties with the provided radios, which are essential for overcoming the gallery's ambient noise and facilitating clear communication. Nonetheless, both my partner, Alysha, and I thoroughly enjoyed the experience. Our guide, Francesco, possessed an impressive depth of knowledge, and his passion for the subject matter was truly contagious. Francesco artfully curated the tour, meticulously selecting a few key artworks that formed a cohesive narrative highlighting the evolution of art in Florence, supported by ample historical context (including some intriguing and scandalous anecdotes—how did a pope end up with a son, one might wonder?). The duration of the tour extended beyond the advertised hour and a half, encompassing approximately two and a half hours. Subsequently, participants are free to explore the gallery further at their leisure.

Doing the Uffizi Gallery Independently

Of course, it is entirely feasible to navigate the Uffizi Gallery independently, and the following section will guide you through the process. However, I highly recommend acquiring the audio guide, as the additional fee is justified by the wealth of insights it provides.

To facilitate your understanding of the ticket procurement process, please note that Uffizi Gallery tickets can be purchased here. The cost per person is 20 Euros, with a reduced price ticket of 2 Euros available for qualifying individuals (details regarding eligibility can be found here, predominantly encompassing E.U. residents aged 18-25).

Foremost, it is crucial to recognize that while advance ticket booking is not mandatory, it is strongly advised, particularly during the summer season. The ticket office queues can be astonishingly long, and entry availability is limited for each time slot.

Naturally, booking tickets in advance incurs an additional cost of 4 Euros per ticket, while also reducing flexibility due to the fixed entry time. Once you have completed the online purchase, a visit to the ticket office is still necessary to exchange the digital ticket for a physical one—a practice that may seem antiquated in the year 2023. Nonetheless, this arrangement affords the benefit of expedited entry, significantly shortening the ticket pick-up queue.

If you choose not to book tickets in advance, be prepared for the longest wait in Florence, as you join the line at the ticket office. Allow me to reiterate the importance of booking tickets ahead of time. Despite the slight added expense and diminished flexibility, the benefits far outweigh these minor inconveniences.

Alternatively, you may consider skip-the-line tickets available through Get Your Guide, facilitating direct access to the security checkpoint (which, although it may entail a short line, moves swiftly).

Tips For Visiting The Uffizi Gallery

Before your visit, it is advantageous to be aware of the following details:

The Uffizi Gallery is closed on Mondays.

Only water bottles with a capacity of 500ml or less are permitted inside (we learned this regulation just before entry, resulting in our rapid consumption of one liter of water).

Larger backpacks must be checked at the coatroom, while smaller backpacks or sling bags may be exempted (for example, my 20L camera bag required checking, whereas Alysha's smaller backpack did not).

Take A Walking Tour To Understand Florence's Rich History

Florence's history is undeniably rich, both in terms of its prosperity and captivating past. As the former banking capital of Europe, Florence played a pivotal role in the minting of the first international currency, the gold florin. This city held great significance, boasting an abundance of remarkable artworks commissioned due to its affluence. Contrary to popular belief, Florence's wealth preceded its artistic heritage, enabling the creation of extraordinary masterpieces.

The enthralling walking tour we experienced shed light on an intriguing perspective shared by our guide, Andrea. He revealed that Florence's artistic abundance was a direct result of its financial prosperity. To truly appreciate the historical context, we recommend partaking in a walking tour that focuses on Florence's connection with the Medici Family, the Holy Roman Empire, and the Catholic Church.

Andrea's Walking Tour of Florence captivated us from the moment we embarked on it during our first evening in the city. Andrea, exuding authentic Italian charm, infused the tour with energy and enthusiasm. The two-hour duration struck a perfect balance, allowing us to delve into the city's history, witness noteworthy sights, and gain essential knowledge to guide our subsequent explorations. The tour commenced at Piazza di Santa Croce, situated on the eastern side of Florence, and concluded at Piazza di San Lorenzo. Along the way, we made stops at Piazza della Signoria to learn about Cosimo I de' Medici, the Grand Duke of Tuscany, and to admire the enduring bronze statue of Perseus, which has graced the same location for over five centuries. This introductory tour comes highly recommended, ideally taken early in your visit to Florence.

While there are numerous other walking tour options available in Florence, we feel compelled to mention an alternative choice: the Take Walks tour of Florence. Having had exceptional experiences with Take Walks in various Italian cities, particularly Rome, we vouch for their expertise in providing engaging tours. This tour follows a similar route to Andrea's, encompassing the city's highlights. However, there are two significant differences. Firstly, the tour commences at 9:15 am on most days, providing an early start compared to Andrea's afternoon tour. Secondly, it includes a visit to the Galleria dell'Accademia di Firenze, where Michelangelo's David stands as the centerpiece. With a duration of three hours, this comprehensive tour offers profound insights into Florence's illustrious history.

See The Most Magnificent Sculpture On The Planet

My first encounter with Michelangelo's David at the Galleria dell'Accademia di Firenze left an indelible impression. This awe-inspiring sculpture is widely regarded as one of the most magnificent artworks in existence. To my surprise, its scale exceeded my initial expectations. Towering at a height of 17 feet,

Georgia Tucker

David's majestic presence looms above spectators, who marvel at the intricate details from below. The colossal undertaking was entrusted to Michelangelo, a native of nearby Santa Croce, in the early 1500s after previous artists had attempted and failed to shape the massive marble block into a lifelike masterpiece.

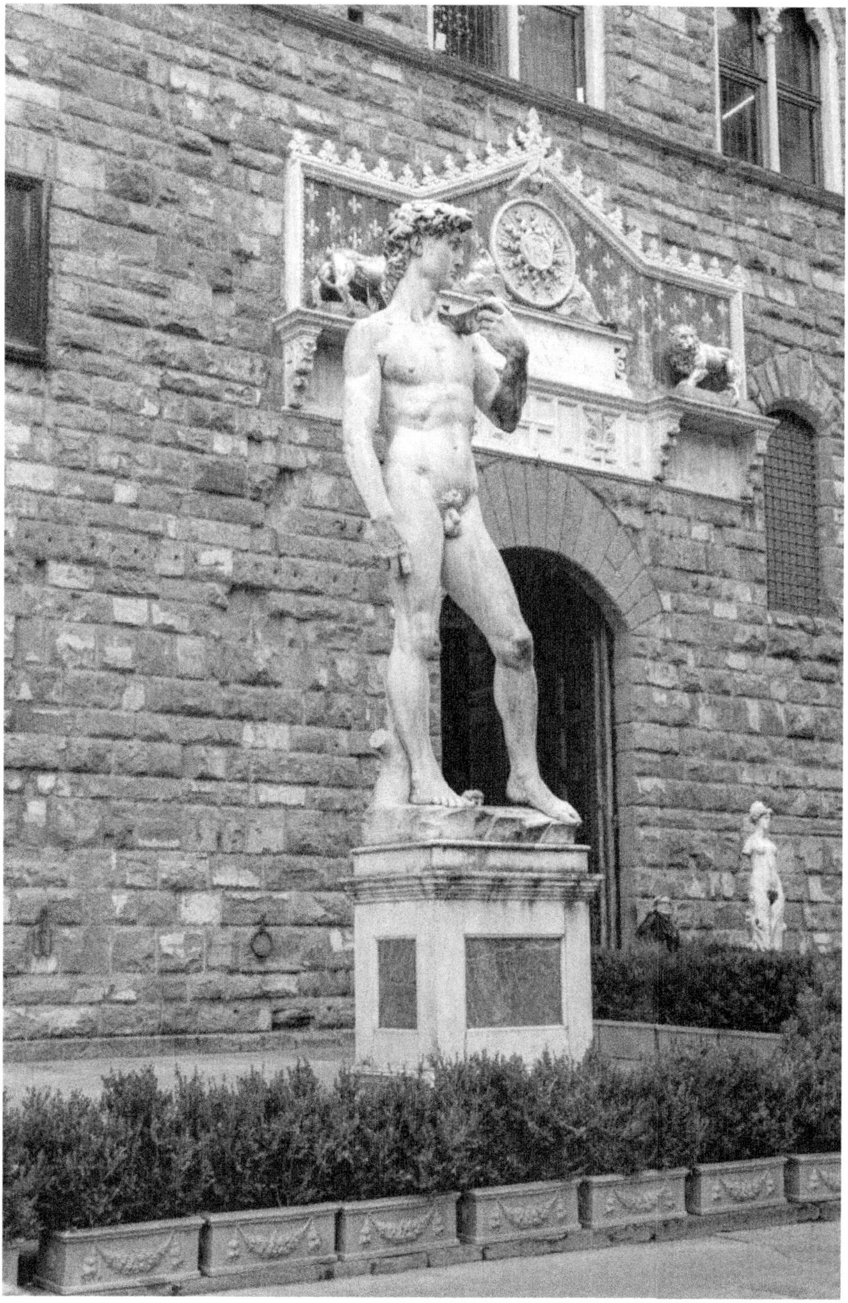

Georgia Tucker

Undoubtedly, the Accademia Gallery ranks among the top three must-see attractions in Florence, alongside the Uffizi Gallery and the Duomo di Firenze, which offers panoramic views from its rooftop and houses captivating artwork within its dome. While the Accademia primarily revolves around the David, it also features a few other notable pieces that warrant exploration. Notably, two replicas of David exist in Florence: one at Piazza della Signoria, outside Palazzo Vecchio, where the original once resided before being relocated to the Accademia, and another at Piazzale Michelangelo.

To visit the Galleria dell'Accademia, you have two options: pre-booking tickets independently (a highly recommended approach) or joining a guided tour. If you choose to secure tickets on your own, it is crucial to note that they tend to sell out several months in advance, especially during peak season, which coincides with the summertime. Thus, booking as early as possible is advisable. If tickets are unavailable due to last-minute planning, opting for a guided tour provides the best opportunity to admire Michelangelo's David.

It is worth mentioning that if you can only accommodate one guided museum tour in Florence, we suggest selecting the Uffizi Gallery. The guided tour there offers a more comprehensive understanding of the art, history, and cultural context surrounding the exhibited masterpieces. This is not to diminish the value of a guided tour at the Accademia; rather, it highlights the enriching experience provided by the Uffizi tour. Please note that the Accademia is closed on Mondays.

Visiting The Galleria Dell'accademia Independently

To ensure a smooth and enjoyable visit to the Gallery, it is advisable to secure tickets well in advance. Once you have determined your dates for Florence, it is recommended to promptly proceed with booking tickets for the Accademia. Detailed information regarding ticket purchases can be found on the official website. We suggest utilizing B Tickets, a reliable platform we have personally used for accessing the Boboli Gardens in Florence. Ticket prices amount to 16 Euros per person, with reduced rates available for EU citizens aged 18 to 25, and free admission granted to individuals under 18 years of age.

Upon selecting a timeslot, representing a 15-minute window allowing entry into the museum, we recommend considering a lunchtime or late afternoon timeslot. These periods typically experience less crowding compared to the morning and early afternoon, which are typically the busiest times for museums in Florence.

Please note that there is a 4 Euro fee for pre-booking tickets. However, we emphasize the importance of this step as it eliminates the need to wait in line both at the ticket office and at the entrance. This convenience makes the additional fee well worth the investment. Alternatively, skip-the-line tickets can be pre-booked, offering a similar price point and avoiding the potential confusion associated with navigating the official website.

Visiting The Galleria Dell'accademia On A Guided Tour

There are compelling reasons to consider a guided tour when planning a visit to the Accademia Gallery. Firstly, if you find yourself arranging your trip to Florence at short notice and discover that tickets for the Gallery are already sold out for your desired dates, a guided tour provides a valuable alternative. Secondly, if you seek a deeper understanding of the story behind the David and its creation, a guided tour can offer the context you desire.

In our own experiences, we have found that opting for guided tours of art museums enhances the overall richness of the visit. The insights provided by experts are truly valuable, ensuring a more meaningful engagement with the artwork. Without such guidance, wandering aimlessly through the galleries can lead to a lack of direction and a missed opportunity to appreciate the narratives behind the art.

Two types of guided tours are available for the Accademia. The first focuses exclusively on the Gallery itself, while the second incorporates the Gallery as part of a comprehensive Florence walking tour. The choice between the two depends on your interests and the itinerary you have planned for your time in Florence.

For those seeking a guided tour solely dedicated to the Accademia Gallery, we recommend selecting a highly reviewed option. These tours often take place around lunchtime, when crowds tend to thin out and offer flexible durations of one or two hours to accommodate different preferences and budgets. For detailed pricing, reviews, and availability, please refer to the provided link.

If you prefer a broader Florence walking tour that includes a visit to the Accademia, we suggest considering Take Walks, a reputable company that we have personally used for multiple tours in Italy. Take Walks offers a VIP David & Duomo tour, encompassing both the Accademia and a climb to the top of the Duomo's dome. To explore pricing, reviews, and availability for this comprehensive tour, please follow the provided link.

Climb 400+ Stairs To The Top Of Brunelleschi's Dome

Before embarking on the ascent to Brunelleschi's Dome, it is crucial to book tickets in advance, as this is a mandatory requirement. Tickets must be purchased beforehand, specifying a specific timeslot for entry.

The price for accessing Brunelleschi's Dome is 20 Euros per person, which may be considered relatively steep, mirroring the challenging nature of the climb. The dome, situated atop the Florence Cathedral, stands as one of the city's most iconic attractions. Every day, numerous visitors gather at Piazza del Duomo to behold the masterpiece crafted by Brunelleschi—a goldsmith by trade during the 15th century, rather than an architect.

However, the reward for reaching the summit is a sublime panoramic view. From the top, visitors are treated to a 360-degree vista of Florence and the picturesque rolling green hills of Tuscany.

Georgia Tucker

Climbing Brunelleschi's Dome: What To Know Before You Go

Ascension to the dome necessitates climbing over 450 stairs, with no elevator or alternate means of access available. The climb entails sections that are steep, narrow, or a combination of both, often shared with a significant number of fellow visitors.

During the ascent, there is a point where visitors traverse a narrow balcony, safely separated by a glass wall, offering a spectacular view of the dome's interior artwork. It is worth taking a moment to admire the intricate details on display. However, due to the limited space and the tendency for congestion as visitors pause to appreciate the view, some individuals may feel uncomfortable in this setting. While Alysha experienced some restlessness after approximately five minutes, Matt, despite a mild aversion to heights, remained at ease.

If you have a fear of heights, claustrophobia, or physical limitations that prevent you from climbing over 450 steps to reach the dome's summit, it is advisable to carefully consider whether this journey is suitable for you. Additionally, bear in mind the associated cost of 20 Euros per person before proceeding with the experience.

Buying Your Tickets For The Dome

It is essential to obtain tickets in advance for ascending the Dome, and they are priced at 20 Euros (10 Euros for reduced-price tickets, subject to eligibility). To purchase tickets for the Dome, please visit the designated website provided. Upon accessing the website, navigate to the "Brunelleschi's Dome" section and select your preferred date and time slot.

Alternatively, for those seeking a more streamlined ticket purchasing process, skip-the-line tickets can be booked through an alternative platform. These tickets provide the same access to the Dome. We strongly recommend selecting an early morning or late evening time slot for optimal lighting conditions, as the panoramic view from atop the Dome during sunset imparts a surreal golden glow (note that this experience is more attainable outside of the summer months when the sun sets earlier).

If tickets are sold out for your desired days in Florence, it is still possible to access the Dome by booking a guided tour. This may be the only viable option at that point. We suggest considering a guided tour that encompasses a two-hour experience, encompassing both the ascent to the Dome and a guided walk around the exterior, providing insights into the cathedral's historical significance.

Wander The Boboli Gardens

Following our visit to the Uffizi Gallery, which coincided with lunchtime, we encountered a considerable queue of individuals eagerly awaiting a culinary delight. Initially assuming it was the line for gallery tickets, we soon discovered that it was, in fact, the line for sandwiches at All'Antico Vinaio. Renowned worldwide and highly reviewed on various platforms, this establishment attracts a constant influx of tourists in search of their famous focaccia sandwiches, which have gained immense popularity to the extent of expanding globally.

Georgia Tucker

Eat A Schiacciata On Via Di Neri

In Florence, these delectable sandwiches are referred to as "Schiacciata." They are a beloved form of street food, as evidenced by the presence of multiple shops with similar offerings, each accompanied by long queues extending onto the street. A Schiacciata typically consists of two pieces of focaccia, which differ from traditional focaccia in terms of preparation and seasoning, enveloping cured meats, cheeses, and various accompaniments.

We had the pleasure of sampling a Schiacciata from Sgrano, a gluten-free restaurant located conveniently down the street. Our selection featured pancetta, gorgonzola, peppers, and honey, and it proved to be a truly delightful culinary experience. This recommendation is not intended as an advertisement for the most famous sandwich shop in Italy, as they undoubtedly receive ample recognition. Instead, we encourage you to visit the street in question during lunchtime and savor a Schiacciata from one of the numerous vendors who offer an array of fillings, encompassing meats, cheeses, vegetables, and even seafood. This option provides an affordable and satisfying lunch, which we recommend enjoying while strolling toward the Arno River, finding a scenic spot overlooking Ponte Vecchio to savor the meal with a captivating view.

Explore The Other Side Of The Arno

Oltrarno, situated just a short walk away from the historical center, emerged as one of our favorite areas in the city. It exudes a slightly calmer ambiance and attracts fewer tourists while offering a vibrant array of excellent restaurants, cafes, and local businesses. Crossing Ponte Vecchio leads you into the "local's Florence," as described by Andrea, our knowledgeable walking tour guide.

The opposite bank of the river boasts a multitude of enticing establishments and warrants dedicating an afternoon to its exploration. For a delightful tour of Oltrarno, we recommend commencing by crossing Ponte Vecchio and proceeding to explore the captivating Boboli Gardens. Enhance your experience by enjoying a cup of coffee at Ditta Artiginale, renowned as one of Florence's finest coffee shops, followed by a visit to Gelateria Della Passera, where Alysha discovered her favorite gelato in Italy, just a short distance away.

Continue your journey to the bustling Piazza Santo Spirito, which offers an excellent vantage point for observing people and immersing yourself in the vibrant atmosphere of Florence. From there, head eastward, passing through the rose garden to reach Piazza Michelangelo, boasting the city's most breathtaking view, albeit shared with numerous visitors at any given time.

Once you have savored the magnificent vistas to your heart's content, descend into San Niccolò and traverse Porta San Niccolò, one of the original city gates, to return to the opposite side of the river.

Explore Two Of Florence's Food Markets
Florence boasts two prominent food markets, each offering distinct experiences that are worthy of exploration.

Mercato Centrale: A Larger, Centrally Located, And Popular Destination

The first market to consider is Mercato Centrale, situated northwest of the Duomo. It encompasses two separate sections—the Mercato di San Lorenzo on the ground floor and the food hall known as Mercato Centrale on the upper level.

Mercato Centrale caters more to tourists and comprises three main components. Outside, an artisan market showcases a variety of stalls offering products ranging from purportedly handcrafted leather goods to phone cases and scarves. Notably, this location holds personal significance as Matt purchased a leather messenger bag from here nearly a decade ago, which he still occasionally uses.

On the ground floor, visitors encounter a combination of fresh produce stands presenting seasonal fruits, and vegetables sourced from Tuscany's fertile farmland, along with butchers, cheesemongers, and specialty shops offering an array of Tuscan delicacies, conveniently packaged for souvenir or gift purposes. While this is an ideal place to purchase items to bring home, it should be noted that prices can be slightly higher, and the authenticity may vary.

The upper floor houses a bustling food hall hosting diverse stalls serving authentic Tuscan cuisine, sushi, and an array of culinary delights. Notably, Pasta Fresca, located in a corner of the market on the lower level, garners significant attention with its handmade portions of pasta, attracting a crowd of pasta enthusiasts. Please note that the ground floor is open from approximately 8:00 am to 2:00 pm, Monday to Saturday, while the Food Hall operates daily from 10:00 am to midnight.

MERCATO SANT'AMBROGIO: MORE LOW-KEY AND LOCAL

Mercato Sant'Ambrogio, comparatively less famous and frequented than Mercato Centrale, offers a delightful experience. We particularly enjoyed our visit to this market and even purchased an assortment of cheeses from one of the vendors to curate our cheese plate at home.

Inside the market, visitors will find a variety of stalls offering fresh ingredients such as meats, fish, and cheeses, as well as ready-to-eat food options. Additionally, the market features an exterior area akin to a farmer's market, where local vendors sell freshly picked produce, providing an authentic glimpse into the local shopping experience. Notably, there is even a stand showcasing an entire fully cooked pig's head, a sight we had not previously encountered. Furthermore, a section of the market resembles a flea market, featuring vendors selling gadgets and clothing.

Mercato Sant'Ambrogio embodies the authenticity of central Florence, with Italian being the predominant language spoken here. Nearby, you'll discover excellent coffee at Coffee Mantra and the best tea shop in Florence, The Way of Tea, located directly across the street from the market. The market operates from Monday to Saturday, 7:00 am to 2:00 pm.

Enjoy The Best (Free) View In Florence At Piazzale Michelangelo

A visit to Piazzale Michelangelo is an absolute must during your exploration of the other side of the river, as previously mentioned.

The view from Piazzale Michelangelo surpasses that of the Duomo's rooftop, mainly because it encompasses the Duomo itself. Located on the hill across the Arno River from Santa Croce, this vantage point offers a breathtaking panoramic vista of Florence, including iconic landmarks such as the Duomo, Palazzo Vecchio, and Ponte Vecchio. This spectacular view attracts an immense crowd, especially during sunset, when hundreds of people gather at this viewpoint.

To make the most of this experience, we recommend an alternative approach: visit Piazzale Michelangelo in the early morning. By doing so, you'll encounter significantly fewer crowds, sharing the space with only a few early risers, fellow runners, and locals who frequent the area. Additionally, the morning light enhances the scenery, with the sun illuminating the Duomo and the Florence skyline from behind, creating optimal conditions for capturing stunning photographs. While there is a replica of the David on the terrace, it is essential to note that it is only a reproduction.

Take A Day Trip – There's A Bunch Of Them!

Florence's central location provides convenient access to a myriad of captivating day trips, allowing you to explore much of Central Italy within a few hours' reach. Wine enthusiasts can embark on a wine tasting tour outside the city limits, delving into the picturesque Tuscan wine country. Two options are available: a guided tour visiting multiple wineries with transportation provided or an immersive experience at a single winery, necessitating self-arranged transport. Both options offer exceptional opportunities to immerse oneself in one of the world's most renowned wine regions.

For food enthusiasts, a visit to Bologna is highly recommended. Widely regarded as one of Italy's best food cities, Bologna offers a gastronomic paradise with its delectable prosciutto, Parmesan cheese, balsamic vinegar, and traditional dishes like tagliatelle alla Bolognese. To witness the charm of Tuscan hilltop towns, consider visiting Siena or San Gimignano. Take Walks, one of our preferred tour companies in Italy offers a comprehensive day trip to Tuscany that includes transportation, visits to both towns, and a wine tasting experience.

During our recent trip, we discovered Verona, which captivated us with its allure. Located approximately 90 minutes away from Florence by high-speed train, Verona is a recommended destination for a day trip, provided you utilize the efficient train

Georgia Tucker

service. To help plan your visit, we have prepared a detailed guide to spending a day in Verona.

Another delightful day trip option is Lucca, where you can embark on a stroll atop the well-preserved medieval walls encircling the city, offering breathtaking views. Please note that Pisa is also accessible; however, we suggest prioritizing the aforementioned options as the leaning tower of Pisa tends to attract large crowds of tourists, making it challenging to capture an exclusive experience.

CHAPTER THREE

GREAT ITINERARIES, 1,2,3 DAYS

FLORENCE IN A DAY: YOUR 10 STOP ITINERARY IN 2023

In a country as rich in cultural heritage as Italy, proper planning becomes paramount. While it may seem that a single day in Florence is insufficient, embarking on a day trip from Rome or Venice offers a remarkable opportunity to experience the city's highlights. This carefully curated itinerary will optimize your limited time. Alternatively, if you prefer a hassle-free experience, consider our Florence in a Day Tour.

We highly recommend dedicating more than a day to fully appreciate the wonders of Florence. However, when time is constrained, it is better to seize the opportunity to explore Florence rather than miss out entirely. This itinerary also serves as an excellent starting point for those spending a weekend or longer in Florence, allowing you to visit prominent landmarks such as the Santa Maria del Fiore Cathedral (Il Duomo), Ponte Vecchio, and Piazza della Signoria.

Immerse yourself in Florence's esteemed Accademia and Uffizi galleries, and indulge in delectable delights at the Mercato Centrale and Gelateria Edoardo. With focused determination, you can explore all these attractions in a single day. Here is your 10-

stop Florence in a Day Itinerary: How to Make the Most of Your Day in Florence.

Stop 1: Getting To Florence

Situated in a central location between Milan, Venice, and Rome, Florence offers convenient accessibility by train. This facilitates the exploration of the city within a day, contrary to initial expectations. We recommend securing your ticket to Florence's Santa Maria Novella Train Station in advance to obtain the most favorable price. Opting for an early train departure ensures ample time to visit all the notable attractions. To check train schedules and fares, please refer to the official Trenitalia website.

Address: Santa Maria Novella Train Station

Stop 2: Accademia Gallery

Located a mere 15-minute walk from Santa Maria Novella Train Station, the Accademia Gallery holds immense popularity due to its prized possession: Michelangelo's David. Arriving before 9:30 am is highly advisable, particularly during peak seasons when significant crowds gather. To guarantee entry and secure the best available rate, we recommend pre-booking tickets online. For a truly enriching experience, consider a Florence tour that includes expert guidance through the gallery, specifically focusing on Michelangelo's David.

Address: Via Ricasoli, 58/60 | Opening Hours: Tuesday – Saturday 8:15 am – 6:50 pm

Stop 3: Mercato Centrale

After immersing yourself in the Accademia Gallery, you are likely to develop an appetite. Embark on an 8-minute stroll to the Mercato Centrale, where you can satiate your hunger. Recharge with a cup of coffee, fresh fruit, or a snack before embarking on a day filled with sightseeing in Florence. The two-floor market offers a diverse selection of fresh Italian produce, allowing you to either pack a picnic lunch or savor a meal in the food court-style setting on the second floor, reminiscent of a local dining experience.

Address: Piazza del Mercato Centrale, Via dell'Ariento | Opening Hours: Monday – Sunday, 9 am – 12 am

Stop 4: Florence Cathedral Of Santa Maria Del Fiore (Il Duomo)

A brief 10-minute walk from the Mercato Centrale leads to the imposing presence of the Duomo, a grand cathedral at the heart of Florence. Construction of this magnificent structure commenced in 1436 and spanned over a century during the peak of the Florentine Renaissance. The exterior showcases an awe-inspiring display of vibrant colors, towering bronze doors, and a remarkable cupola or dome.

You have the option to enter the cathedral free of charge or purchase a comprehensive €18 ticket, granting access to Brunelleschi's Dome, Giotto's Bell Tower, the Baptistry of San Giovanni, the Crypt of Santa Reparata, and the Opera Museum. Please consult the official website for accurate opening hours, as they may vary depending on the season and religious holidays. To enhance your experience, we recommend a guided tour with an expert who can provide valuable insights. Our skip-the-line Florence Duomo tour, including a dome climb and access to the secret terraces, guarantees an unparalleled view of Florence's crown jewel.

Address: Piazza del Duomo | Admission Cost: Free entry to the Cathedral; €18 for special areas ticket

Stop 5: Gelateria Edoardo

Were you aware that Florence is the birthplace of gelato? A family-owned establishment renowned for its authentic flavors, Gelateria Edoardo awaits just a 3-minute walk from the Duomo. This delightful shop presents organic gelato crafted using century-old recipes. For an extraordinary indulgence, savor their hand-made cones generously adorned with multiple scoops of gelato.

Address: Piazza del Duomo, 45/R | Opening Hours: 11:30 am – 11 pm

Stop 6: Ponte Vecchio

Following a gratifying culinary experience, embark on a 9-minute stroll to Ponte Vecchio, one of Florence's oldest landmarks. This iconic bridge stands as the sole crossing point over the Arno River that remained intact during World War II, as the Germans chose to dismantle the surrounding structures instead. Notably, the bridge features shops integrated into its structure, many of which specialize in jewelry and gold. Do not miss the opportunity to witness this captivating architectural marvel during your visit to Florence.

Address: Ponte Vecchio

Stop 7: Piazza Della Signoria And The Uffizi Gallery

A mere 4-minute walk from Ponte Vecchio lies Piazza della Signoria, an outdoor art gallery that adds to the splendor surrounding the Uffizi Gallery. This remarkable square is adorned with statues, monuments, and fountains, while also hosting the Palazzo Vecchio, currently serving as Florence's town hall.

Your next destination is the renowned Uffizi Gallery, home to a wealth of extraordinary artworks, including Botticelli's Birth of Venus. Opting for a guided tour of the Uffizi Gallery can greatly enhance your visit. We offer a selection of highly-rated tours that breathe life into the gallery's masterpieces.

Stop 8: Basilica Of Santa Croce

A brief 10-minute walk from Piazza della Signoria leads to the remarkable Basilica di Santa Croce. Notable for being the final resting place of esteemed figures such as Michelangelo and Galileo, this stunning church offers a captivating blend of culture and history within its surrounding piazza. Take advantage of the picturesque setting to capture memorable photos and engage in leisurely people-watching moments. To avoid queues, we recommend pre-booking tickets in advance, as opening hours may vary depending on the season and religious holidays.

Address: Piazza di Santa Croce, 16 | Opening Hours: Monday – Saturday, 9:30 am – 5:30 pm; Sunday, 12:30 pm – 5:45 pm

Admission Cost: €8 for adults, while children under 18 accompanied by paying parents enjoy free entry. Individual tickets for visitors aged 12 – 17 years cost €6.

Stop 9: All'antico Vinaio

Regrettably, your Florence day trip is drawing to a close. If hunger strikes and you desire a delectable snack for the train journey, make a stop at All'Antico Vinaio, renowned for its Florentine panino sandwiches. With an extensive array of choices, the friendly servers are more than willing to provide suggestions at this popular street food destination. A beloved option is the porchetta or pork sandwich paired with a glass of Tuscan wine. Buon Appetito!

Address: Via dei Neri, 74/R

Stop 10: Fontana Del Porcellino

En route to the train station, take a moment to visit Il Porcellino, a bronze pig fountain with fascinating folklore associated with it. It is believed that rubbing the pig's nose before departing Florence ensures a safe return. Another tale suggests that your wish will be granted if you place a coin inside the Porcellino's mouth, allowing it to cascade down into the grate below. These coins are utilized to support a local orphanage, making your participation in this tradition a benevolent conclusion to your Florence day trip. From here, you may proceed to your hotel or the train station. Arrivederci!

Address: Piazza del Mercato Nuovo

Take A Florence In A Day Tour

If you prefer the guidance of an expert during your exploration of Florence, we encourage you to explore our Florence in a Day tour. This comprehensive tour includes skip-the-line access to the Accademia and Uffizi Galleries, accompanied by an expert guide. Additionally, you will embark on a walking tour of Florence, allowing you to intimately encounter renowned landmarks such as the Duomo, Palazzo Vecchio, Ponte Vecchio, and the district associated with Dante's upbringing.

YOUR COMPLETE 3-DAY FLORENCE ITINERARY

While there are numerous remarkable attractions to experience in Florence, it is essential to prioritize your choices, particularly when limited to a three-day visit. This guide aims to assist you in determining the key highlights to focus on while leaving room for future explorations.

Florence is best savored at a leisurely pace. While it is undoubtedly important to visit iconic sites like the Uffizi Gallery and other renowned landmarks, it is equally vital to allocate time to savor the splendid culinary delights and wines of Tuscany, as well as to stroll along the charming riverbanks.

An enchanting aspect of Florence is its ideal position as a base for venturing into the surrounding wonders of Tuscany. On your third day, we highly recommend embarking on a day trip to the captivating destinations of Lucca, Bologna, or the esteemed wine region of Chianti.

Here's what the itinerary looks like at a high level.

Day 1: Exploring Brunelleschi's Dome, an Introduction to Florence, and the Statue of David

Day 2: Visit the Uffizi Gallery and Exploration of Oltrarno

Day 3: Customizable Day Trip Experience

Assuming your arrival the evening before, you have three full days at your disposal to delve into the wonders of Florence. If you're planning a trip to Italy, our comprehensive guide to crafting an unforgettable Italy itinerary is a valuable resource. It offers insights and suggestions for one-week, ten-day, and fourteen-day itineraries, tips for organizing your trip effectively, and an array of must-see attractions and activities along the way.

Day 1: Brunelleschi's Dome, An Introduction To Florence, And The Statue Of David

Embark on your first day by ascending to the summit of Florence's Duomo, immersing yourself in the city's history, and concluding with a visit to the renowned Statue of David.

Brunelleschi's Dome And The Florence Cathedral

Commence your exploration early on the first day of this Florence itinerary to experience the main attractions at Piazza del Duomo before the crowds swell. This square houses several significant landmarks, including the iconic Duomo, the Baptistery, and Giotto's Campanile. The architectural unity of these structures, characterized by their Gothic-Renaissance style and renowned marble design, is striking.

We highly recommend focusing on one attraction within the complex rather than attempting to visit all of them. In particular, Brunelleschi's Dome stands out for several reasons. First, it offers the finest panoramic view of Florence from its summit, unlike the Campanile, which has netting obstructing photography. Second, it provides an up-close encounter with the cathedral's most captivating interior feature, the dome, thereby bypassing the long queues to access the cathedral's interior.

If you wish to explore all the attractions on Piazza del Duomo, purchasing a combined Duomo complex ticket will save you both time and money. Alternatively, guided tours of the Duomo complex are also available.

OPENING TIMES FOR KEY ATTRACTIONS ON PIAZZA DEL DUOMO:

- Campanile: 8:15 am to 6:45 pm

- Baptistery: 8:15 am to 10:15 am and 11:15 am to 7:30 pm

- Duomo Museum: 9:00 am to 7:00 pm (closed on Sunday afternoons)

- Duomo: 10:00 am to 4:30 pm

- Brunelleschi's Dome: 8:30 am to 5:00 pm

Climbing Brunelleschi's Dome

The awe-inspiring Gothic-Renaissance cathedral, dating back to the 13th century, stands as one of the world's largest Christian churches. However, the true highlight of the Duomo lies in its magnificent dome, famously known as Brunelleschi's Dome, which was once the largest of its kind globally.

Take a moment to appreciate the intricate exterior adorned with remarkable sculptures and designs. Upon entering the cathedral, you will notice a relatively simpler interior, though the vast marble floor leaves a lasting impression. Ascend to the dome's pinnacle for a close-up view of its remarkable frescoes and a breathtaking panorama of Florence. To optimize lighting conditions and minimize crowds, we strongly recommend purchasing tickets for the 8:15 am time slot and arriving in line by 8:00 am.

Georgia Tucker

It's An Early Morning, But We Think It's Worth It.

Though an early start, we believe the experience justifies the effort. Tickets for the Dome can be purchased through the official website, where you can select "Brunelleschi's Dome," choose a date and time slot, and proceed with the booking. Alternatively, if you prefer to avoid any potential complexities associated with the official website, you can secure skip-the-line tickets, which provide the same access to the Dome.

Reaching the dome's summit involves climbing 463 steps, as there is no elevator available. The pathways leading to the top are somewhat narrow and confined, making it less suitable for individuals with severe claustrophobia. At a certain point, you will traverse along a narrow balcony, safely enclosed by a glass wall, hovering high above the church floor—a truly spectacular sight.

From this vantage point, you can marvel at the intricate art adorning the interior of the dome, particularly the depictions of heaven and hell. Some of the figures portrayed in the hell section evoke curiosity about the artistic inspirations of that era. The sheer imagination manifested in this masterpiece is truly captivating.

While pausing to admire the artwork, it is important to note that other visitors will likely do the same. Standing on a narrow ledge, several hundred feet above the ground, may not be suitable for everyone. Alysha, for instance, experienced some restlessness after approximately five minutes, prompting me to mention this. Personally, despite a slight aversion to heights, I felt perfectly at ease throughout the experience.

A Walking Tour

Engaging in a guided walking tour stands as our preferred approach to acquainting ourselves with a newly discovered city upon arrival. Consequently, we wholeheartedly suggest dedicating the initial morning of this three-day Florence itinerary, following the ascent of the dome, to this immersive experience. By partaking in such a tour, not only will you gain a comprehensive understanding of the city's layout and the whereabouts of its principal attractions, but you will also delve into Florence's captivating past and enjoy the invaluable opportunity to seek insights from a well-informed local guide.

While various walking tours of Florence serve as suitable introductions to the city, we present a specific recommendation based on our encounter in Florence. During our inaugural evening in the city, we embarked on Andrea's Walking Tour—an exceptional venture that truly stood out among the various walking tours we experienced during our extensive three-month journey throughout Italy, Spain, and Portugal. Andrea epitomizes the essence of an Italian host, radiating an authentic energy and enthusiasm that deeply resonated with us. His tour provides an exceptional overview of the city, spanning a concise duration of two hours. This timeframe allows for a thorough immersion into Florence's rich history, offering glimpses of iconic landmarks and equipping visitors with the necessary knowledge to efficiently allocate their time or revisit specific sites in the future, all while ensuring a seamless and engaging experience.

Commencing from the eastern side of the city, specifically Piazza di Santa Croce, the tour navigates its way to Piazza di San Lorenzo, encompassing notable stops along the route. Of

Georgia Tucker

particular significance is Piazza della Signoria, where participants can absorb insights into the life and legacy of Cosimo I de' Medici, the esteemed Grand Duke of Tuscany while beholding the enduring bronze statue of Perseus, an emblematic presence that has graced the same location for over five centuries.

We wholeheartedly recommend Andrea's Walking Tour as an exceptional introduction to Florence, advising visitors to partake in this endeavor as early as feasible during their visit. Additionally, we would like to highlight a few other notable walking tours in Florence that serve as excellent avenues for familiarizing oneself with the city's essence.

Firstly, we propose the "Best of Florence Tour" by Take Walks, a captivating small-group excursion lasting two hours and thirty minutes. If you have previously perused our Rome guides, you are likely aware of our admiration for Take Walks (for further details, we invite you to explore our extraordinary Colosseum tour). This Florence-based tour comprehensively covers the historical narratives and anecdotes of the city's prominent highlights, ranging from the iconic Ponte Vecchio bridge to the resplendent Florence Duomo, among many other noteworthy attractions. Furthermore, the tour conveniently incorporates a skip-the-line entry to behold Michelangelo's masterpiece, David, housed within the Florence Accademia—a well-curated itinerary that accomplishes multiple objectives within a single undertaking.

Secondly, we endorse the "Introduction to Florence" tour offered by Context Travel, featuring a duration of three hours and thirty minutes. Guided by a local historian, this immersive journey acquaints participants with Florence's principal sites and neighborhoods while unveiling the city's enthralling historical narrative. As an added highlight, the tour includes an opportunity to witness the awe-inspiring statue of David and explore the captivating Accademia Gallery, further enriching the cultural and artistic experience.

Lunch At Mercato Centrale (San Lorenzo Market) Or Sant'ambrogio Market

Florence boasts a pair of vibrant food halls, each offering distinct experiences. Both options present favorable choices for a satisfying lunch amidst your sightseeing activities, although the San Lorenzo Market holds an advantage in terms of its convenient location for the day's itinerary.

The San Lorenzo Market, also known as Mercato Centrale, comprises two levels: the lower level is dedicated to fresh produce like fruits, vegetables, cheeses, and meats, while the upper level houses a trendy food hall replete with a diverse array of stalls and culinary options. Additionally, an outdoor market complements the indoor sections, featuring an assortment of leather goods, trinkets, and other appealing gadgets.

The Food Hall Portion Of San Lorenzo Market

Alternatively, the Sant'Ambrogio Market draws a local crowd engaged in their weekly shopping, particularly on Saturdays. Here, a more intimate yet authentic selection of stands await, encompassing butchers, cheesemongers, and vendors offering ready-to-eat delicacies.

For an enhanced gastronomic experience, we recommend embarking on a guided food tour that incorporates visits to these markets, allowing you to savor local delicacies under the guidance of an expert.

The Statue Of David And The Accademia Gallery

The Accademia Gallery undoubtedly ranks among the top three must-see attractions in Florence, alongside the Uffizi Gallery and the awe-inspiring Duomo di Firenze, offering captivating perspectives from its roof and showcasing remarkable artwork inside its dome.

Upon witnessing the statue of David for the first time, I was struck by its sheer magnitude. Contrary to my prior assumption of it being life-sized, the statue stands an impressive 17 feet tall. While the Accademia Gallery predominantly revolves around the splendor of David, it also boasts a few other notable art pieces that deserve your attention.

To visit the Galleria dell'Accademia, you have two main options. You may choose to independently pre-book tickets (and we strongly recommend doing so), or you can opt for a guided tour. If you decide to secure tickets on your own, be aware that they sell out months in advance during peak season, particularly in the summertime. Therefore, it is advisable to secure your tickets as early as possible. If you are planning a last-minute trip and find tickets unavailable, joining a guided tour presents the optimal solution to experience the magnificence of David.

Please note that the museum is closed on Mondays, thus necessitating proper planning to align your visit accordingly.

DAY 2: THE UFFIZI GALLERY AND EXPLORING OLTRARNO

The second day of your itinerary is filled with exciting activities, commencing with a visit to one of the world's most beloved art museums, the Uffizi Gallery, followed by an exploration of the charming neighborhood of Oltrarno, and culminating with an unforgettable panoramic view of Florence.

Santa Croce Church (Basilica Di Santa Croce)

Embark on your day with a brief stop at the Basilica di Santa Croce. This Gothic-Renaissance church, although slightly detached from the other prominent attractions (a mere 5-10 minute walk away), is well worth a visit due to its status as the final resting place of numerous esteemed Italians. Among the illustrious figures interred here are the renowned artist Michelangelo, who called the Santa Croce neighborhood home, as well as the eminent scientist Galileo Galilei and the influential political philosopher Niccolò Machiavelli. The church also houses an impressive collection of artworks.

A highlight of the church is its facade, which, when observed from various angles, appears to have been added to enhance its visual appeal from the front. Other sections of the church exhibit a more austere and less ornate design, underscoring its transformation over the years from a humble place of worship to one of Florence's significant religious landmarks.

Georgia Tucker

Piazza Della Signoria

While Florence boasts numerous picturesque squares, Piazza della Signoria stands out as the city's main square and an absolute must-visit destination.

Keep An Eye Out For:

- The Fountain of Neptune

- Cosimo I de' Medici on horseback, one of the most important figures in the sometimes salacious history of Florence

- A replica of Michelangelo's David – don't let anyone convince you it's the real one! – in the place where the original used to stand before being moved indoors out of the elements

- The many lifelike statues of important historical figures like Galileo and Da Vinci along the Loggia dei Lanzi

Piazza della Signoria is also home to Palazzo Vecchio, the historic seat of government in Florence and a significant architectural landmark that is impossible to miss.

A History Of Renaissance Art At The Uffizi Gallery

Conclude your second afternoon in Florence by visiting another iconic attraction, the Uffizi Gallery. Located just south of Piazza della Signoria, this world-renowned gallery houses an unparalleled collection of Renaissance and European art, painstakingly amassed by the influential Medici family during their centuries-long reign as Florence's prominent figures.

As the birthplace of the Renaissance, Florence, and the Uffizi Gallery in particular, is an absolute must-visit for art enthusiasts.

The gallery proudly exhibits countless priceless masterpieces by renowned Italian artists, including Botticelli's "The Birth of Venus," Michelangelo's "Doni Tondo," and Leonardo da Vinci's "Annunciation." With a staggering 101 rooms and a vast array of artworks to explore, a visit to the Uffizi Gallery warrants a minimum of a few hours. However, deciding where to focus your attention amidst this vast collection can be challenging.

This is where a guided tour proves invaluable, a choice we made. Just as we enjoy guided tours at notable museums like the Louvre in Paris and the Vatican in Rome, expert guides provide invaluable context and insight that often elude us when navigating these museums independently. Without their guidance, we would simply glance at the artwork and move on, appreciating only their superior's beauty without comprehending the historical and cultural significance that underlies each piece.

We Believe That A Guided Tour Is Worth It For A Few Reasons.

Given the gallery's immense size, unless you possess a deep knowledge of art history, having someone curate the artwork and highlight the key artists and pieces becomes essential.

An art historian brings two crucial elements to the experience: historical and cultural context (providing insights into the artist and the world during the creation of each masterpiece) and storytelling. These elements breathe life into the artworks, enabling you to understand their profound significance in the history of Florence and Italy at large.

The skip-the-line access is another advantage. The ticket queues are consistently long, and whether you choose a guided tour or not, we strongly advise pre-booking your tickets to bypass the lines and proceed directly to the security checkpoint. fully booked a guided tour of the Uffizi Gallery in Florence and thoroughly enjoyed the experience.

Independent Visit: If you prefer to explore independently, we highly recommend investing in an audioguide. As one of the city's most popular and busiest attractions, it is crucial to book your ticket and time slot online in advance. Entrance slots are available in 15-minute intervals until 5:00 pm daily, and the museum remains open until 6:50 pm, allowing ample time for exploration even if you arrive in the late afternoon.

Lunch At Via Dei Nei

Upon exiting the Uffizi Gallery onto Via dei Neri, we were taken aback to find ourselves amidst a lengthy queue. Speculating about the purpose of this line, we walked alongside it, curious to uncover the source of anticipation. At its forefront, we encountered an unexpected sight.

This line was for a sandwich, but not just any sandwich. It was for a "Schiacciata" from All'Antico Vinaio, an internationally renowned food establishment. The Schiacciata, a popular form of street food in Florence, consists of two pieces of distinctively prepared focaccia, generously filled with cured meats, cheese, and other accompaniments.

Visitors have a choice to either join the queue for the famous establishment, explore alternative nearby options that pique their interest, or venture a short distance down the street to Sgrano, a gluten-free restaurant offering a 100% gluten-free version of the sandwich. After securing their chosen sandwich, they can enjoy it on the banks of the Arno River before proceeding to Ponte Vecchio for a memorable crossing.

Ponte Vecchio

Merely a brief two-minute walk from the Uffizi Gallery lies the renowned Ponte Vecchio, a historic bridge that spans the Arno River. Distinguished by its unique appearance, it stands as Florence's oldest bridge and a survivor of the World War II bombings. Since the 13th century, the bridge has been adorned with shops, although their nature has evolved over time. Originally housing butchers and fishmongers, the banishment of their malodorous presence has led to the predominance of high-end goldsmiths and jewelers today.

While you may catch glimpses of Ponte Vecchio during your exploration of Florence, we recommend experiencing it in the evening when it begins to illuminate with a captivating glow. As most of the shops close by then, taking a stroll across the bridge, observing the wooden shutters and back, ng in the sunset views along the Arno River, evokes a sense of romance. Don't forget to look up and admire the Vasari Corridor, an elevated passageway constructed by the Medici family to enable them to traverse without mingling with the common populace.

Oltrarno: A Self-Guided Walking Tour

Between Ponte Vecchio and the Boboli Gardens, take the opportunity to explore the neighborhood on the opposite side of the river, which offers an array of delightful food, beverages, and charming piazzas deserving of your attention. While we provide a suggested route on the map, we encourage you to embark on your discoveries.

Here Are Some Stops We'd Recommend Based On Our Own Experience.

Ditta Artigianale: This established specialty coffee shop in Florence, with its newer location, boasts a beautiful interior and a pleasant outdoor patio. The coffee served here is exceptional.

Gelateria Della Passera: Alysha's favorite gelato in Florence, if not all of Italy. Situated on a charming square, it offers a perfect spot to relax, savor gelato, and engage in people-watching. Piazza Santo Spirito: As mentioned by Andrea, the walking tour guide, this lively piazza is a local hangout. With the Basilica Santo Spirito on one end and a lovely fountain on the other, the square is lined with bars and restaurants, providing an ideal setting to bask in the sunlight and pass the time.

Le Volpi e l'Uva: Among our cherished wine experiences in Florence, this venue offers a wide selection of Italian wines from Tuscany and other regions. The passionate staff is eager to engage in discussions about various grape varieties and their current wine recommendations.

The Boboli Gardens

After enjoying a glass or two of wine, proceed up the street to Pitti Palace. However, if time is limited, we do not recommend visiting the palace (included in the "with more time" section below). Instead, focus on the enchanting green space behind the palace known as the elegant Boboli Gardens. Separate tickets are available exclusively for the gardens at a significantly lower cost.

Encompassing a vast area of over 45,000 square meters, the gardens constitute the largest green expanse in Florence. As you leisurely wander through the grounds, you will encounter fountains, pergolas, grottos, a small lake, and numerous ornate Renaissance statues. It serves as a serene retreat from the bustling city outside.

The View From The Boboli Gardens
On a pleasant day, we recommend bringing along some beverages, such as an Aperol Spritz, and snacks to relish a late lunch or afternoon aperitivo as a picnic in the tranquil gardens.

Note: The entrance to the gardens is the same as the entrance to Pitti Palace. If you face Pitti Palace, the ticket office is situated to the right. To avoid lengthy queues, we advise obtaining your tickets in advance. While you can skip the line with electronic tickets, please note that paper tickets must be collected before entry, a detail that surprised us.

Piazzale Michelangelo
Conclude your day on the opposite side of the river by ascending to the most remarkable vantage point in the city, Piazzale Michelangelo. Join the gatherings of both locals and tourists who ascend to Piazzale Michelangelo, offering the most breathtaking sunset panoramas in the city.

Situated atop a sizable hill, this expansive terrace features a bronze replica of Michelangelo's renowned David sculpture. It is crucial to note that the replica should not be mistaken for the original. Additionally, the location encompasses a restaurant and numerous vendors that cater to the influx of visitors that frequent this stunning destination to admire the views each evening.

From Le Volpi e l'Uva, you can reach Piazzale Michelangelo with a leisurely 20-minute walk. En route, you will pass through the rose garden, a worthwhile pause to appreciate the blossoming roses during spring and summer. The stroll offers splendid panoramic vistas.

Should you prefer not to walk, you may opt to board bus line 12, which will transport you to the summit. The bus can be accessed from the southwestern end of Boboli Gardens at Porta Romana (available on Google Maps).

Dinner At Mister Pizza Or Ciro And Sons

On your second evening in Florence, it is time to savor the delights of pizza. During our five-week stay in Italy, we indulged in copious amounts of pizza, despite Matt's requirement for a gluten-free diet due to his Celiac Disease.

Two establishments in Florence are highly recommended for their pizza offerings, including gluten-free options. Our preferred choice was Mister Pizza, which boasts two locations within the city center. One is conveniently situated beneath the Duomo, allowing patrons to dine while enjoying a view of the dome. The second location, nestled towards Santa Croce, provided us with a serene lunch experience on our final day in Florence.

Ciro and Sons, although a few blocks away from the main attractions in Florence, does not compromise on culinary excellence. However, it is worth noting that the main challenge lies in the substantial queues and occasionally disorganized staff. Consequently, we found ourselves waiting in line (more accurately, a clustered mass of people) for over an hour, even with a prior reservation. While the pizza is commendable, it did not rank as our favorite in Florence.

DAY 3: CHOOSE YOUR DAY TRIP

On your last day in Florence, capitalize on the city's strategic location at the heart of the picturesque Tuscany region by embarking on a day trip to one of the remarkable nearby destinations.

You may be contemplating visits to Pisa and Cinque Terre; however, we advise against both as day trips from Florence for various reasons.

Pisa fails to impress beyond its iconic leaning tower. Furthermore, the city is swarming with tourists. Interestingly, Bologna, which offers an alternative day trip, also features a leaning tower—a recommendation we endorse. Cinque Terre, on the other hand, is too distant to comfortably explore within a day and warrants more time for a comprehensive experience.

Instead, we propose considering a day trip to Bologna, celebrated as one of the finest culinary destinations in Italy, especially appealing to gastronomy enthusiasts who relish prosciutto, parmesan, and bolognese cuisine. Alternatively, Lucca, a captivating town with well-preserved medieval walls, or the Chianti wine region are equally alluring options.

Georgia Tucker

OPTION 1: BOLOGNA – THE CHOICE FOR FOODIES

For food connoisseurs visiting Florence, Bologna tops our list of recommendations. Renowned within Italy and across Europe, Bologna captivates with its culinary heritage. Fortuitously, we were accompanied by friends who had relocated from the United States to Bologna, and they graciously provided us with an immersive introduction to the Emilia-Romagna region. This region is renowned for gastronomic delights such as tagliatelle al ragu (resembling pasta Bolognese but distinct from the American perception), parmigiano reggiano, prosciutto di Parma, balsamic vinegar from Modena, and mortadella.

In essence, a day trip to Bologna is an absolute must for those seeking to savor some of the finest cuisine Italy has to offer.

Getting To Bologna

Reaching Bologna from Florence is a straightforward journey, facilitated by a high-speed train departing from Florence's Santa Maria Novella Station. The travel time typically spans approximately 40 minutes, delivering you to Bologna Centrale. From the station, it is a mere 20-minute walk to the principal attractions in Bologna.

What To Do In Bologna
Walk, Eat, Repeat.

Essentially, the itinerary revolves around walking and indulging in culinary delights. Ascend the Torre degli Asinelli: Did you know that Bologna boasts its very own leaning tower, albeit less renowned than its Pisa counterpart? Scaling the heights of Torre degli Asinelli rewards visitors with magnificent vistas encompassing Bologna and its surroundings.

Culinary exploration: Commence your gastronomic journey at the Quadrilatero, an extensive area situated just east of the main square, Piazza Maggiore. This district teems with remarkable eateries, vibrant market stalls, and charming shops offering an array of meats, cheeses, and delectable provisions. A noteworthy stop would be Mercato di Mezzo, a bustling food hall boasting diverse culinary options. Our personal experience led us to Tamburini, a gourmet grocery store, where we procured prosciutto and parmesan to savor later in Florence.

OPTION 2: LUCCA – A BEAUTIFUL TOWN WITH MEDIEVAL WALLS

Lucca presents an excellent day trip opportunity for those desiring an authentic Tuscan town experience that diverges from the more frequented cities of the region, such as Florence and Siena. Despite its lesser-known status, Lucca radiates the distinctive charm inherent to Tuscany.

Located west of Florence, toward the coast, Lucca traces its roots back over 2,000 years to its founding by the Etruscans before becoming a Roman settlement. Notably, Lucca boasts an intact set of medieval city walls, a rarity in contemporary times.

Georgia Tucker

Getting To Lucca

Allow us to present the good news and the bad news for this particular excursion. The good news is that traveling from Florence to Lucca is both convenient and cost-effective.

Regrettably, the journey entails a regional train, which operates at a slower pace, resulting in a lengthier travel time. The fare amounts to 10 Euros each way, with direct trains departing approximately once an hour, requiring around one hour and twenty minutes.

What To Do In Lucca

Embark on a circumnavigation of the city atop its walls: Our most treasured activity in Lucca was strolling along the entirety of the city walls, covering a 4-kilometer distance. This enchanting journey bestows a unique experience while affording captivating views of Lucca. During our visit in autumn, the surroundings were adorned with the vibrant hues of the season. Engaging in this delightful endeavor serves as a perfect prelude to exploring the center of Lucca.

Ascend the tower: Torre Guinigi, situated in the heart of Lucca, offers an intriguing feature—a small garden atop the tower. From this vantage point, visitors are treated to breathtaking 360-degree vistas encompassing the city and the distant mountains. Climbing 230 steps leads to the summit, positioned 145 feet above the ground.

Piazza dell'Anfiteatro: Take a stroll through the old medieval center of Lucca, with Piazza dell'Anfiteatro serving as an excellent starting point. This public square once housed a Roman amphitheater and retains its amphitheater-like shape to this day.

Unwind amidst the sun-drenched ambiance, enjoy a glass of wine or an espresso, and replenish your energy before further exploration.

OPTION 3: CHIANTI – TASTE SOME OF THE BEST WINE IN THE WORLD

For wine enthusiasts, Tuscany offers an unparalleled destination. Renowned as one of the world's most celebrated wine regions, it is easily accessible from Florence for a memorable day trip. Chianti, in particular, stands out with its bold and robust red wines, prominently featuring esteemed grape varieties such as Sangiovese and Barolo. Wineries located just outside Florence provide an opportunity to indulge in the finest offerings.

To fully enjoy a day trip into the wine country, we recommend opting for a guided tour, ensuring a seamless experience. Although an independent excursion is possible with a rental car, joining a group tour offers distinct advantages, allowing you to savor the exceptional wines without concerns about transportation.

You have two enticing options to consider. The first entails a tour that includes visits to multiple wineries and convenient transportation arrangements. Alternatively, you may choose to immerse yourself in a more in-depth experience with a single winery, arranging your transportation to and from the destination. The former option eliminates the need to navigate trains and buses, while the latter offers a more economical alternative, albeit requiring additional logistical planning. Regardless of your choice, both options provide an opportunity to explore one of the world's most renowned wine regions.

Georgia Tucker

WHAT TO DO WITH MORE TIME IN FLORENCE

If you find yourself with additional time in Florence, we suggest considering the following attractions to enhance your visit:

Pitti Palace (Palazzo Pitti)

Pitti Palace, an exquisite Renaissance palace dating back to the 15th century, houses a series of museums and galleries. It served as the principal residence for the ruling families of the Grand Duchy of Tuscany.

The Palace Is Now Split Into Four Main Museums:

The Treasury of the Grand Dukes

The Palatine Gallery and the Imperial and Royal Apartments

The Gallery of Modern Art

The Museum of Costume and Fashion

While exploring the entire palace could easily occupy an entire day, we recommend focusing on the opulent Appartamenti Reali and the Costume Gallery for a leisurely couple of hours. The Costume Gallery showcases a stunning collection of clothing, featuring notable brands like Gucci, Versace, and Prada. While individual tickets can be purchased for each museum, we suggest considering the Passepartout combination ticket for the Pitti Palace, Boboli Gardens, and Uffizi Gallery, which offers cost savings (€38).

The Campanile Di Giotto (Giotto's Bell Tower)

The Campanile di Giotto, a freestanding bell tower adjacent to Florence's Duomo, stands as an impressive architectural marvel. Designed in the 14th century by the renowned painter Giotto di Bondone, after whom it is named, the tower rises to a remarkable height of 277.9 feet. Although Giotto passed away before its completion, it took two additional architects 25 years to finalize the construction.

To reach the tower's pinnacle, one must ascend the steep 414 steps, as there is no elevator available. Despite the physical exertion, the climb is well worth it, as it offers breathtaking views of Piazza del Duomo and the panoramic splendor of Florence. The Campanile opens at 8:15 am, and early arrival is recommended to avoid crowds.

The Baptistery (Battistero Di San Giovanni)

Situated near the Campanile, the Florence Baptistery is regarded as one of the oldest structures in the city. While many visitors admire its exterior, we highly recommend venturing inside to marvel at the extraordinary Byzantine ceiling mosaic dating back to the 12th century.

A notable highlight of the Florence Baptistery is the "Porta del Paradiso" (Gates of Paradise). It is important to note that the current gates are replicas, with the original gates preserved in the nearby Museo dell'Opera del Duomo (Cathedral Museum). The combined ticket provides access to the Cathedral Museum, allowing you to view the authentic gates even if time is limited.

However, if you have more leisurely hours to spare, we encourage you to explore the captivating museum extensively.

The Baptistery opens at 8:15 am, but please be aware that it closes temporarily between 10:15 am and 11:15 am each day. Thus, arriving early enables you to visit both the Campanile and the Baptistery between 8:15 am and 10:15 am.

Even More, Things To Add To Your Florence Itinerary

In addition to the aforementioned attractions, here are a few more recommendations to consider for your Florence itinerary: Medici Chapels: Within the Basilica of San Lorenzo, the Medici Chapels serve as the final resting place for many notable members of Florence's influential Medici family. Designed in part by Michelangelo, these chapels offer a remarkable artistic experience.

Strozzi Palace: Concealed within an impressive courtyard, the 15th-century Strozzi Palace now hosts contemporary art exhibitions, providing a unique blend of historical and modern artistic expressions.

San Marco Museum: Housed within a former convent, this museum boasts the largest collection of sacred art in Florence, offering a captivating exploration of the city's religious and artistic heritage.

Piazza della Repubblica: With additional time at your disposal, immerse yourself in the vibrant ambiance of Florence's numerous lively squares, known as piazzas. Piazza della Repubblica, in particular, stands out as a bustling square where you can relish a cup of coffee or a spritz while observing the city's vibrant energy. By including these recommendations in your Florence itinerary, you will create a comprehensive and enriching experience, further embracing the city's cultural, historical, and artistic treasures.

2 DAYS IN FLORENCE ITINERARY

Florence Itinerary Day 2
Uffizi Gallery, Ponte Vecchio & Piazzale Michelangelo

Today, your itinerary encompasses a visit to the magnificent Uffizi Gallery, one of the world's premier art museums, followed by an exploration of Florence's gardens and panoramic viewpoints.

9:30 Am: The Uffizi Gallery

The Uffizi Gallery is renowned not only as one of Italy's most significant art museums but also as one of the world's largest. Its extensive collection consists of thousands of Renaissance artworks generously donated to Florence by the Medici family. Established in 1865, the Uffizi Gallery stands as one of the oldest museums globally and houses masterpieces by renowned artists such as Leonardo da Vinci, Botticelli, Cimabue, Michelangelo, Titian, Raphael, and Caravaggio.

To optimize your visit to the Uffizi Gallery, consider arriving early at 8:15 am, affording you ample time to explore other attractions in Florence, such as the Bargello Museum. Alternatively, for a more relaxed pace, aim to visit around 9:30 am.

How To Visit The Uffizi Gallery:

Make a reservation in advance, selecting a time slot between 8:15 am and 10:00 am, aligning with this itinerary's schedule. Plan for a duration of approximately 2 hours for your visit.

Admission Fee: €20 from March 1 to October 31, €12 from November 1 to February 28, or included with the Firenze Card.

Opening Hours: 8:15 am to 6:30 pm, closed on Mondays.

Website: Reserve your visit online in advance through the official Uffizi Gallery website or via GetYourGuide. At the time of our last check, GetYourGuide allowed cancellation up to 24 hours in advance with a full refund.

Optional: The Bargello

The Bargello Museum is an art museum located in the oldest public building in Florence. It showcases additional Renaissance masterpieces by artists such as Michelangelo, Ghiberti, and Donatello, as well as exhibits of ceramics, tapestries, coins, and armor. Art enthusiasts will find the Bargello Museum particularly rewarding. If you choose to include it in your itinerary, start your visit at 8:15 am, spending approximately an hour and a half there before walking to the Uffizi Gallery, where you can spend the remainder of the morning. Consider booking a 10:30 am entrance ticket to the Uffizi Gallery.

How To Visit The Bargello Museum

Opening Hours: Monday, Wednesday, Thursday, Friday, and Sunday from 8:15 am to 1:50 pm (last entry at 1:00 pm), Saturdays from 8:15 am to 6:50 pm.

Admission Fee: €9 plus a €3 booking fee.

Website: Consult the official Bargello Museum website for up-to-date information on opening hours and pricing.

12:00 Pm: The Vasari Corridor & Ponte Vecchio

While optional, the Vasari Corridor offers a unique and hidden gem experience in Florence. It is an elevated, enclosed walkway constructed in 1565 to connect Palazzo Vecchio with Palazzo Pitti, enabling the Grand Duke to travel between the two. Passing through the Uffizi Gallery, the corridor traverses the church of Santa Felicita and extends over the famous Ponte Vecchio. Historically closed to the public, the Vasari Corridor underwent significant restoration and is set to open to visitors sometime in 2023, exclusively accessible through guided tours.

If a tour of the Vasari Corridor does not align with your plans, take a leisurely walk along the Arno River to Ponte Vecchio, a medieval stone bridge renowned for its jewelry shops.

1:00 PM: Lunch At Signorvino Firenze

Indulge in a delightful lunch at Signorvino Firenze, an exceptional restaurant nestled within a wine shop on the banks of the Arno River, offering splendid views of Ponte Vecchio. To ensure an optimal experience, we recommend making a reservation in advance and requesting a table on the outdoor terrace.

2:30 PM: Gardens In Florence

This afternoon presents an opportunity to explore various gardens in Florence, each offering unique features and stunning city vistas. You can choose to visit all or select one or two, keeping in mind that traversing between them requires some walking, including uphill sections. These gardens are located on the south side of the Arno River.

Boboli Gardens & Pitti Palace

Situated behind the Pitti Palace, Boboli Gardens showcases a multitude of Renaissance statues and fountains, complemented by panoramic views of Florence.

HOW TO VISIT THE PITTI PALACE AND BOBOLI GARDENS:

Admission Fee: €6 for Boboli Gardens, €10 for Pitti Palace, or €14 for a combined ticket, which is also included in the Firenze Card.

Opening Hours: Boboli Gardens opens at 8:15 am, with closing times varying by season. Pitti Palace is open Tuesday through Sunday from 8:15 am to 6:30 pm.

Website: Refer to the official websites of Boboli Gardens and Pitti Palace for the most up-to-date information on hours and pricing. Reservations are required on Saturdays and public holidays.

The Bardini Gardens

The Bardini Gardens, also known as Giardino Bardini, encompass the Renaissance garden of Villa Bardini and offer a serene and less crowded alternative to the bustling Boboli Gardens. Situated on the same hill as the Boboli Gardens, the Bardini Gardens may be smaller in size, but their elevated location provides a superior vantage point for panoramic views of Florence. A visit to the gardens entails two main activities: leisurely strolling through the well-maintained grounds and exploring the villa, which houses various art exhibits. Of particular note is the terrace atop the villa, which affords visitors breathtaking vistas of Florence.

Within the Bardini Gardens, the Wisteria pergola is a must-see attraction. Imported from China by Marco Polo, the wisteria blooms in April and May, adding beauty to the surroundings throughout the year.

HOW TO VISIT THE BARDINI GARDENS:

Access to the gardens is through Villa Bardini.

From Signorvino Firenze, a 7-minute uphill walk along Costa San Giorgio (passing by the house of Galileo Galilei) leads to the Bardini Gardens.

From the Boboli Gardens, it is a brief 5-minute walk along Via del Forte di S. Giorgio to reach Villa Bardini.

Tickets for the Bardini Gardens cost €10 and are included in the ticket for the Boboli Gardens. Advance reservations are necessary for visits on Saturdays, Sundays, and holidays. The gardens are open daily from 10 am to 8 pm, while the villa is open from

Tuesday to Sunday, also from 10 am to 8 pm. For the latest updates, please consult the official website.

Rose Garden

The Rose Garden, also referred to as Giardino delle Rose, offers a captivating viewpoint of Florence and admission is free.

To reach the Rose Garden from the Bardini Gardens, a pleasant 1.3 km walk that takes approximately 20 minutes is required. Enter through Autorita Di Ambito Ato Toscana Centro on Viale Giuseppe Poggi. Exploring the garden itself takes only a few minutes. Upon concluding your visit, follow the path that leads up the hillside to Piazzale Michelangelo.

PRO TRAVEL TIP: If you plan to visit the Pitti Palace, Boboli Gardens, Bardini Gardens, and the Rose Garden, allocate approximately 3 hours for this excursion, adjusting as needed based on the time spent at each location.

5:30 Pm: Piazzale Michelangelo & San Miniato Al Monte

Piazzale Michelangelo stands out as one of the premier vantage points in Florence to witness the mesmerizing sunset. The timing of sunset varies depending on the season, ranging from approximately 6:30 pm (spring and fall) to 9 pm (early summer). If you intend to experience the sunset at Piazzale Michelangelo during the summer months, adjustments to this itinerary, such as allocating more time at the gardens, starting the day later, or visiting San Miniato al Monte before Piazzale Michelangelo, will be necessary.

San Miniato Al Monte

Situated on one of Florence's highest points, San Miniato al Monte is a basilica that commands panoramic views of the city. Located on the hillside above Piazzale Michelangelo, it takes around 10 minutes to reach this site on foot. Apart from savoring the remarkable vistas from the terrace, visitors have the opportunity to explore the interior of the church and wander through the adjacent cemetery.

Piazzale Michelangelo

Piazzale Michelangelo offers breathtaking views of Florence throughout the day. If your visit falls between early May and late July, sunset times generally range from 8 to 9 pm. Given the later timing, consider having an early dinner before proceeding to Piazzale Michelangelo, ideally arriving approximately one hour before sunset. Alternatively, you can begin your evening at a rooftop bar and subsequently take a taxi to Piazzale Michelangelo.

Alternatively, you may choose to visit Piazzale Michelangelo in the late afternoon, relish the panoramic vistas, and then return to the city center via taxi for dinner, possibly while enjoying sunset views from another rooftop restaurant. To ensure optimal timing, consult sunset times for accurate planning. Piazzale Michelangelo can be a popular attraction, especially for those seeking sunset photography, so arriving at least an hour in advance is advisable to secure a favorable viewing spot.

Once you conclude your visit to Piazzale Michelangelo, you can either walk back to the city center or hire a taxi. If sunset occurs at 9 pm, the estimated return time to the city center would be between 9:30 and 10:00 pm.

FLORENCE ITINERARY DAY 1

The Duomo, Michelangelo's David, Palazzo Vecchio & Rooftop Bars

On your first day in Florence, explore the main attractions in the historic city center, including a visit to the iconic Florence Cathedral, with opportunities to ascend both the dome and Arnolfo Tower. Along the way, take advantage of the chance to enjoy a few rooftop bars.

Please note: If you plan to follow this itinerary on a Monday, please skip Mercato Centrale and reschedule your visit to the Accademia Gallery for the following day, as both are closed on Mondays. Similarly, on Sundays, you won't have access to the main floor of the Duomo or be able to climb the dome until 12:45 pm.

To utilize the interactive map provided, click the tab located in the top left corner to view different layers, including the suggested places to visit and the walking route. By clicking the check marks, you can hide or reveal specific layers. Additional information about each point of interest is available by clicking the icons on the map. Moreover, you have the option to save this map to your Google Maps account by clicking the star next to the title. To access it on your phone or computer, open Google Maps, click the menu button, go to "Your Places," select "Maps," and you will find this map on your list.

Morning: The Duomo Complex

The Florence Cathedral, known as the Duomo di Firenze and Cattedrale di Santa Maria del Fiore, stands as one of the world's most recognizable cathedrals. It is part of the larger Santa Maria del Fiore monument complex, which includes the Opera del Duomo Museum, the bell tower, the dome of the cathedral, the baptistery, and Santa Reparata. All these sites are situated nearby on Piazza del Duomo.

When visiting the Duomo complex, several ticket options are available. We recommend purchasing the Brunelleschi Pass, which grants access to all the sites within the complex, including the dome climb. Plan for approximately 4 hours to explore all the attractions thoroughly. For a comprehensive guide to visiting the Florence Cathedral, complete with photos and detailed information about each site, please refer to our dedicated guide. It also provides useful insights if you prefer to prioritize specific sites.

Opening Times At The Duomo Complex

Dome of the Cathedral: 8:15 am from Monday to Saturday; 12:45 pm on Sundays

Main Floor of the Cathedral: 10:15 am from Monday to Saturday; closed on Sundays

Santa Reparata: 10:15 am

The Baptistery: 8:30 am

Opera del Duomo Museum: 8:30 am

Giotto's Bell Tower: 8:15 am

It is advisable to begin your visit at the Opera del Duomo Museum or Giotto's Bell Tower when they open. These sites tend to attract larger crowds later in the day, with more visitors arriving around 9 am. For the dome climb, it is necessary to book a time slot in advance, eliminating the need to queue early since you can arrive at your designated time. It is recommended to secure your booking several weeks ahead of your visit to Florence.

The order in which you visit the sites can be customized, but the following sample itinerary allows for a comprehensive exploration of the Duomo complex:

8:30 am: Opera del Duomo Museum

9:30 am: Dome climb (pre-booked time slot)

10:30 am: Baptistery

11:00 am: Giotto's Bell Tower

11:45 am: Main floor of the cathedral and Santa Reparata. Entry to the cathedral often involves a short line, but it tends to move quickly. Once inside, you can access Santa Reparata by descending the stairs on the main floor.

1:00 Pm: Walk To San Lorenzo Market

By reserving your dome climb early, you can use the remaining morning hours to explore the sites that interest you most. If you prefer a guided tour of the Florence Cathedral, we recommend a highly-rated option that includes entrance tickets and a dome climb.

For a comprehensive understanding of each site within the Duomo complex, available ticket types, and helpful tips, refer to our Florence Cathedral Guide.

Lunch: Mercato Centrale

From the Duomo Complex, it is just a 6-minute walk to San Lorenzo Market.

San Lorenzo Market comprises two sections: an outdoor market and an indoor market located within the Mercato Centrale building. The outdoor market offers a range of leather goods, pottery, and souvenirs and operates from Tuesday to Saturday. Inside Mercato Centrale, embark on a culinary journey through Italy, exploring the various small shops and gathering food for a delightful picnic lunch.

2:00 Pm: Accademia Gallery

Proceed to the Accademia Gallery, located just a 7-minute walk away. The Accademia Gallery, also known as Galleria dell'Accademia, is renowned for housing Michelangelo's iconic masterpiece, the Statue of David. Originally situated on Piazza della Signoria, the statue was relocated to the gallery in 1873.

The Statue of David stands as an exceptional work of art, recognized worldwide for its unparalleled brilliance. Within this small museum, visitors can also admire other works by Michelangelo as well as paintings by Florentine artists. A visit typically takes around 30 to 45 minutes.

Georgia Tucker

How To Visit The Accademia Gallery

To avoid long ticket lines, it is recommended to make an advance reservation online. We suggest booking the earliest available time slot.

Cost: €12 + €4 online reservation fee; included with the Firenze Card

Hours: 8:15 am – 6:50 pm; closed on Mondays

Website: For further information and to purchase tickets in advance, please visit the official website.

Additional Ticket Sellers: GetYourGuide offers entry tickets, and guided tours of the gallery are also available. As of our last update, tickets purchased through the GetYourGuide website could be canceled up to 24 hours in advance, with a full refund.

3:00 Pm: Piazza Della Repubblica

After your visit to the Accademia Gallery, take a pleasant 10-minute stroll to Piazza della Repubblica. Along the way, you will pass by the magnificent Duomo, Florence's cathedral.

Piazza della Repubblica is a significant square in Florence, offering a variety of charming cafes where you can pause for a break and enjoy a delightful meal or refreshing beverage. In the center of the square, a carousel adds a touch of joy, particularly appealing to children. For a remarkable view of Florence Cathedral, two rooftop bars are worth visiting.

Tosca & Nino, located atop the Rinascente department store on Piazza della Repubblica, is a rooftop bar and restaurant that provides fantastic views of the Florence Cathedral. Reservations are not required, and they serve drinks and lunch. Here is a glimpse of the view.

One block away is View on Art, a smaller rooftop bar with an even more captivating view of the Duomo. Please note that service can be slow at times, and the food has received mixed reviews. Nonetheless, it is a splendid place to relax for approximately 30 minutes, savor a drink, and appreciate the breathtaking panorama of Florence.

You have ample time to visit both locations if you wish. However, we have additional rooftop bars on our list for later in the day.

4:00 Pm: Palazzo Vecchio

A 5-minute walk from Piazza della Repubblica leads you to Piazza della Signoria, where Palazzo Vecchio is situated. En route, you will pass by the Fontana del Porcellino. According to legend, rubbing the nose of the boar ensures a return visit to Florence in the future.

Piazza della Signoria is a grand open square that faces Palazzo Vecchio. On the square, you can admire the Loggia dei Lanzi, an open-air sculpture gallery, a replica of the statue of David, and the Neptune Fountain. While here, consider ascending the Arnolfo Tower on Palazzo Vecchio for one of the finest panoramic views of Florence. This viewpoint is among our personal favorites, as it provides an awe-inspiring vista of the Duomo.

How To Visit Palazzo Vecchio:

Cost: Museum €12.50, Tower €12.50, combined ticket €17.50; included with the Firenze Card

Tower Hours: April 1 to September 30: 9 am – 7 pm; October 1 to March 31: 9 am – 7 pm (closing time on Thursdays is 2 pm); last admission is one hour before closing

For further details on hours, guided tours, and ticket purchases, please visit the official website.

5:30 Pm: Aperitifs & Dinner

In Florence, dinner typically commences around 7:00 pm. However, 5:30 pm presents an ideal time for an aperitif. An aperitif is a pre-dinner drink accompanied by a selection of small snacks or a charcuterie board. One of the prime locations to indulge in an aperitif is a rooftop bar. For a comprehensive list, consult our guide to the Best Rooftop Bars in Florence.

Divina Terrazza, a short walk from Piazza della Signoria, offers a more relaxed ambiance and boasts stunning views of the Duomo. Angel Roofbar is also within proximity to Piazza della Signoria. Although the views are not as remarkable as those from Divina Terrazza, they provide an excellent vantage point of Palazzo Vecchio.

B Roof is another noteworthy rooftop bar in Florence, offering splendid views of the Florence Cathedral. Afterward, you can savor a delectable dinner at the B Roof Restaurant, situated atop the Grand Hotel Baglioni, which affords spectacular views of the Duomo.

Following your aperitif, enjoy a delightful dinner in Florence. One highly recommended option is Trattoria Il Bargello, where we enjoyed a satisfying lunch (although it is equally suitable for dinner). This casual restaurant offers excellent pasta dishes at reasonable prices. And of course, remember to save some room for gelato!

CHAPTER FOUR

BEST LOCAL DISHES AND DRINKS FROM FLORENCE

The culinary treasures of Florence embody a remarkable blend of tradition, expertise, and passion. The locals take immense pride in preserving a culinary culture rooted in simplicity and freshness while honoring the rich historical legacy associated with their gastronomy.

Georgia Tucker

Exploring Florence unveils a captivating array of tantalizing Tuscan dishes, each with its unique narrative, visiting this Italian region an absolute delight for food enthusiasts. Regardless of one's budget or culinary preferences, this comprehensive guide to Florence's finest local dishes serves as an ideal starting point for anyone contemplating a journey to the culinary capital of Tuscany.

Fagioli All'uccelletto
Tuscan-Style Baked Beans

Fagioli all'uccelletto, Tuscan-style baked beans, holds a special place in Florentine folklore as a simple yet satisfying vegetarian dish with deep-rooted historical origins. The abundance of beans in the Tuscan region is evident in many local Florence dishes featuring legumes in various forms.

This delightful dish combines Italian borlotti beans, slow-cooked in a hearty tomato sauce infused with distinctive hints of sage and garlic. Served alongside thick slices of crispy Tuscan bread, it offers diners the opportunity to partake in the Italian tradition of Scarpetta, relishing every last bit of sauce remaining on the plate.

Schiacciata
Classic Tuscan Flatbread

Schiacciata, a traditional Florentine flatbread, boasts a crisp and chewy texture, thanks to generous amounts of salt and olive oil incorporated into its preparation. The basic recipe calls for just five ingredients: salt, olive oil, water, flour, and yeast.

Schiacciata takes on various forms, sometimes enjoyed on its own as a midday snack, occasionally topped with cheese and herbs, and during the grape harvest season, filled with fruits for a delightfully sweet treat. There are few culinary pleasures as comforting as freshly baked bread, and Florentine locals have perfected the art of crafting impeccable oven-fired flatbread.

Georgia Tucker

Lampredotto
Florentine Offal Sandwich

The humble lampredotto, a Florentine offal sandwich, harks back to an era when peasants sought to utilize every part of the animal, leaving nothing to waste. Reflecting the culinary principles of cucina povera, the cuisine of the poor, this sandwich showcases the use of the cow's stomach lining.

Typically slow-cooked in a flavorsome broth, the tender and succulent lampredotto is served in a panini, accompanied by a choice of spicy or herby sauce. This Florentine street food staple has withstood the test of time, continuing to delight travelers who visit this paradise for gastronomy.

Bistecca Alla Fiorentina
Florentine Steak

The bistecca alla Fiorentina, or Florentine steak, stands as Florence's most renowned local dish, distinguished by its strict criteria for achieving the prestigious label. To qualify as a true Florentine steak, it must be a T-bone cut weighing between 1 kg and 2 kg, sourced from grass-fed Chianina cows raised on neighboring Sienese farms.

The bistecca alla Fiorentina is traditionally cooked rare, with minimal seasoning of salt and pepper. The charred exterior and rare-cooked meat may divide the opinions of eager carnivores, but one thing is certain: this iconic Florentine dish offers an unforgettable culinary experience.

Coniglio Arrosto Morto
Roasted Rabbit

Similar to many other local dishes found in Florence, the appeal of coniglio arrosto morto lies in its simplicity. Although the presence of rabbits may surprise some travelers, the slow cooking process renders the meat tender and flavorful, resembling chicken with a subtly sweeter taste.

Despite its modest list of ingredients, this Florentine delicacy unveils a delightful blend of flavors. Best savored during the cooler months, the hearty vegetables and rich white wine sauce offer a warm and satisfying experience.

Pappa Al Pomodoro
Tuscan Bread Soup

Pappa al Pomodoro, a Tuscan bread soup, dates back to the 19th century and remains a cherished favorite among both locals and visitors to this region of Italy. Traditionally served cold as a starter during the summer, this soup incorporates passata, a thick tomato paste, along with olive oil, basil, and garlic to infuse it with flavor. The soup's texture is derived from unsalted Tuscan bread simmered within.

During medieval times, pappa al pomodoro helped prevent the wastage of stale bread. This comforting dish exemplifies the ingenuity of Florentine farmers and peasants in transforming simple ingredients into satisfying culinary creations.

Tagliatelle Funghi Porcini E Tartufo
Truffle and Porcini Mushroom Tagliatelle

Locally sourced porcini mushrooms and delectable Tuscan truffles take center stage in this renowned Florentine dish. The earthy flavors of truffle shavings harmonize with the meaty texture of porcini mushrooms, resulting in a pasta dish that deserves the attention of every traveler in Florence.

Tagliatelle ribbons, longer and flatter than fettuccine, are tossed in a creamy mushroom sauce and garnished generously with parsley to complement the distinctive flavors of the fungi. As mushroom production peaks between August and October, the freshest truffle and porcini mushroom tagliatelle can be savored in Florence during the mid-autumn season—an irresistible combination that will leave you yearning for more.

Pappardelle al Cinghiale
Wild Boar Ribbon Pasta

Pappardelle al cinghiale, a renowned dish in Florence, offers visitors a delightful culinary experience. Wild boar, a versatile game meat, takes center stage in this dish, prepared through various methods, including curing and cooking. The boar is typically marinated overnight in red wine, stewed in a savory tomato sauce, and served atop wide, ribbon-like pasta known as pappardelle. Apart from its health benefits as a lean alternative to pork, wild boar is also a sustainable choice, with a population of over 150,000 roaming the national parks of Tuscany. While its texture is often compared to venison or pork, marinating, and slow cooking tenderize the meat, resulting in a flavorful and succulent dish.

Fiori Di Zucca Ripieni
Stuffed Zucchini Blossoms

Fried squash blossoms, known as fiori di zucca ripieni, represent a delectable appetizer that should not be missed during your visit to Florence. These delightful morsels are popular not only in Tuscany but across Italy. The squash blossoms are delicately coated in rice flour batter and then either pan-fried or deep-fried until they acquire a golden and crispy exterior. The true delight lies within, as the blossoms are generously filled with a decadent ricotta cheese mixture, although some variations substitute it with anchovy and mozzarella. This local specialty is irresistibly scrumptious and serves as an excellent introduction to your main course.

Georgia Tucker

Crostini di Fegatini
Chicken Liver Crostini

Crostini di fegatini, a versatile Florentine appetizer with its origins in the Tuscan farming community, is a culinary delight. Typically, this dish consists of toasted baguette slices or bruschetta, generously topped with a luscious and buttery chicken liver pate. However, we recommend exploring various toppings, such as capers, anchovy paste, or salsa, as they beautifully complement the crispy crostini. With numerous variations of this Florentine staple available, we encourage you to indulge in a variety of options, ensuring you savor the best local flavors Florence has to offer.

Cocktail
Negroni

The Negroni, a classic cocktail, is crafted by combining equal parts gin, sweet vermouth, and Campari. While its exact origins remain somewhat uncertain, it is widely believed that Count Camillo Negroni invented this cocktail in Florence back in 1919. Seeking to enhance his favorite drink, the Americano, the Count replaced soda with gin, creating the beloved Negroni. The cocktail gained immense popularity, prompting the Count to produce a ready-made version in a distillery. Known for its bitter profile, the Negroni is typically served over ice in an old-fashioned glass, garnished with an orange wheel, and enjoyed as an apéritif.

Olive Oil
Chianti Classico

Chianti Classico, an olive oil distinct from the renowned wine varietal, originates from the Colline del Chianti, a picturesque range of hills nestled in the heart of Tuscany, between Florence and Siena. This central Tuscan extra virgin olive oil boasts a maximum acidity of 0.5% and displays a vibrant yellow hue with hints of green. The Frantoio, Correggiolo, Moraiolo, and Leccino olive varieties contribute approximately 80% of the olives used in the production of Chianti Classico. These olives are meticulously hand-picked and promptly pressed within three days of harvesting to ensure optimal flavors. Due to its sensitivity to heat, Chianti Classico extra virgin olive oil is best savored raw, drizzled over traditional Tuscan dishes, or utilized in salad dressings, adding a delightful touch to the culinary experience.

Georgia Tucker

Herbal Liqueur
Alchermes

Alchermes, an ancient Italian liqueur, is a blend of rosewater, orange blossom water, sugar, herbs, and spices. Traditionally, its characteristic red hue is derived from the inclusion of crushed cochineal insects. The origins of this liqueur are attributed to the Sisters of the Order of Santa Maria dei Servi in Florence. Presently, numerous brands offer Alchermes, with many using artificially derived dyes to achietheirits distinctive red color. With its subtle spiciness, Alchermes can be savored as a digestif or employed in the creation of delightful sweets. Notably, it finds a place in traditional desserts like pesche di Prato and zuppa Inglese, an Italian trifle-like delicacy, as well as inspiring the zuppa Inglese gelato flavor.

THE BEST RESTAURANTS IN FLORENCE

Florence is renowned for its exquisite cuisine, characterized by rich flavors, simple yet impactful ingredients, and a distinct personality. One cannot explore the city's culinary scene without indulging in the queen of Florentine dining—the Bistecca. Be sure not to miss our recommendations for the best steaks to savor in the city.

When discussing restaurants in Florence, it is impossible to overlook the beloved trattorias. These establishments embody the soul of the city, skillfully combining the true flavors of a cuisine that speaks the language of tradition. It is here that iconic dishes like ribollita and pappa al pomodoro were born.

Another cherished Florentine tradition is that of the "buche," cozy and distinctive restaurants nestled in the cellars of ancient buildings. Here, the rich Tuscan cuisine comes to life with flavors that explode on the palate—succulent steaks, truffles, mushrooms, and other delicacies, all accompanied by excellent wines.

When culinary excellence beckons, Florence answers. We have curated a selection of must-try restaurants in the city center, encompassing a diverse range of cuisines, including traditional, elegant, pizzerias, Michelin-starred establishments, seafood-focused venues, vegetarian and gluten-free options, as well as Oriental and international fare.

Georgia Tucker

If you're planning a trip beyond Florence, we also provide recommendations for restaurants located on the outskirts of the city.

Now, let's explore some of the outstanding restaurants in Florence:

La Fiorentina Osti
Address: Via del Trebbio, 1/r

Contact: +39 055 213768

Description: La Fiorentina Osti showcases an open kitchen and rustic ambiance, embodying the essence of Tuscan cuisine. The walls adorned with posters narrate the restaurant's history when travelers would stop by for a glass of wine and a bowl of tripe served on a newspaper. The menu boasts a wide range of dishes, including charcoal-grilled steak, homemade pasta, and delectable desserts. Open for dinner as per regular evening hours.

Buca Lapi
Address: Via dei Girolami, 28/r

Contact: +39 055 213619

Description: Buca Lapi, one of the smallest buche in Florence, has been serving customers since 1945. Notable dishes include ribollita, Sangiovannese stew, fried chicken, rabbit, artichokes, and their cult-favorite artichoke pie (served in winter and spring) and pork arista with roasted potatoes. Conclude your meal with candied baked pears. The restaurant accommodates up to 40 seats indoors and outdoors.

Buca Mario

Address: Piazza degli Ottaviani, 16/r

Contact: +39 055 214179

Description: Buca Mario preserves the simplicity and genuineness of Florentine cuisine through its use of authentic ingredients and traditional recipes. Highlights include artichoke flan, ribollita, pappardelle with wild boar sauce, and grilled steak. During winter, ossobuco (marrow bone) and lombatina (loin of pork) with artichokes are among the must-try dishes. The restaurant offers a private room with a back exit and has a maximum capacity of 140 seats along with small outdoor dehors. Open for dinner every evening and for lunch on Saturdays and Sundays.

Cammillo

Address: Borgo San Jacopo, 57/r

Contact: +39 055 212427

Description: Cammillo stands as a testament to a Florentine culinary heritage, featuring charcoal-grilled Florentine steak and an array of delectable fried dishes. Their handmade tortellini, a legacy of Bruno from Bologna, and the exotic shrimp curry with rice and homemade mango chutney have been served since the 1950s. The restaurant proudly offers organic oil and wine from the farm Il Peraccio, owned by Chiara's brother, Francesco. Cammillo also provides an extensive selection of vegetarian and gluten-free options. Closed on Wednesdays.

Georgia Tucker

Coco Lezzone

Address: Via del Parioncino, 26/r

Contact: +39 055 287178

Description: Coco Lezzone is a typical Florentine trattoria, evoking the atmosphere of the early 1900s with its checked tablecloths, friendly conversations, and portraits of renowned artists and celebrities adorning the walls. The menu features signature dishes such as pappa al pomodoro, ribollita, roast pork, and an excellent steak marinated in olive oil, salt, and pepper before cooking. The restaurant is open for both lunch and dinner, accommodating around thirty guests indoors. Closed on Sundays and Tuesday evenings.

Il Magazzino

Address: Piazza della Passera, 2/3

Contact: +39 055 215969

Description: Il Magazzino offers an array of delightful dishes, including lampredotto meatballs, ravioli stuffed with lampredotto and potato, linguine with black cabbage pesto, and Florentine tripe. Their extensive wine list boasts 180 labels, and don't miss the Lampredotto with porcini mushrooms. The restaurant can accommodate up to 28 seats indoors and 6 seats outdoors. Opening hours vary, with Monday and Tuesday serving lunch only, and Wednesday to Sunday offering lunch from 12:00 to 15:00 and dinner from 19:00 to 23:00.

Il Santo Bevitore

Address: Via S. Spirito, 64/r

Contact: +39 055 211264

Description: Situated in the heart of Oltrarno, Il Santo Bevitore offers a contemporary yet intimate atmosphere with candlelit charm. The menu highlights include terrine of chicken livers with Vin Santo and pan brioche and beef tartare with crispy vegetables. The restaurant caters to celiac and vegetarian diets, and its wine list is extensive and carefully curated. For an aperitif, visit Santino, a small wine shop adjacent to the restaurant. Il Santo Bevitore can accommodate up to 50 seats indoors and 25 seats outdoors. Opening hours are from 12:30 to 14:30 for lunch and from 19:30 to 23:00 for dinner.

La Giostra

Address: Borgo Pinti, 10/12/18r

Contact: +39 055 241341

Description: La Giostra, founded two decades ago by Prince Dimitri d'Asburgo Lorena and his son Soldano, is an intimate and hidden gem frequented by celebrities worldwide. The restaurant offers an exclusive round table reminiscent of King Arthur's table, where you can indulge in cult dishes like Carbonara di Tartufo Bianco or Filetto con Funghi Porcini. La Giostra provides a main dining room with 46 seats and a secondary dining area with 49 seats. Opening hours are from 12:30 to 14:30 for lunch (Monday to Friday) and from 19:00 to 24:00 for dinner (Monday to Sunday).

Georgia Tucker

Trattoria Da Sostanza, Known as Il Troia
Trattoria Dei 13 Gobbi

Address: Via del Porcellana, 9/r

Phone: +39 055 284015

Trattoria Da Sostanza, widely recognized as Il Troia, showcases its culinary expertise through its renowned specialties. Indulge in the incomparable rigatoni served in a transparent soup tureen and savor the inevitable sliced beef presented on a wooden log. Complementing these delectable dishes is an extensive wine list featuring the finest labels. Moreover, the trattoria accommodates various dietary preferences, offering dedicated menus for celiac and vegetarian patrons. With its versatile offerings, Trattoria Da Sostanza ensures an exceptional dining experience for all guests, available for both lunch and dinner.

Trattoria Dei 13 Gobbi
Trattoria Gargani

Address: Via del Moro, 48/r

Phone: +39 055 2398898

Trattoria Dei 13 Gobbi, a favored meeting spot for artists and intellectuals, exudes a lively and convivial ambiance with its embellished walls. Presently led by Chef Elio Cotza, who has been an integral part of this establishment from its inception, and joined by Andrea Gargani, the trattoria continues its exciting culinary journey. The menu boasts cult favorites such as spaghettino with raw artichokes, escalope with avocado, and the legendary cheesecake. Trattoria Dei 13 Gobbi captivates diners with its gastronomic delights and engaging atmosphere, embodying the essence of a memorable dining experience.

Trattoria Mario

Address: Via Rosina, 2r

Phone: +39 055 218550

Established in 1953 and proudly family-run for nearly four generations, Trattoria Mario resides within a sixteenth-century building known as Palazzo Alessandri. Immerse yourself in the evocative atmosphere of Tuscan heritage, as the trattoria sources strictly fresh Tuscan products each morning from the Central Market, enveloping the space with their enticing aromas. Traditional specialties, including the renowned ribollita, Florentine steak, peposo, and lampredotto, are showcased on the menu. Operating for lunch every day except Sunday, and additionally open for dinner on Wednesday through Saturday, Trattoria Mario warmly welcomes guests to savor their authentic Tuscan fare.

Cucina Torcicoda

Address: Via Torta, 5r

Phone: +39 055 2654329

Situated near Piazza Santa Croce and a stone's throw away from Ponte Vecchio, Cucina Torcicoda offers a unique gastronomic experience within the heart of Florence. Its contemporary setting strikes a harmonious balance between tradition and modernity. The establishment features both a pizzeria equipped with a wood-burning oven and a gourmet restaurant where one can relish the unmissable Florentine steak. A meticulously curated wine cellar houses an extensive selection of over 300 labels. Reflecting their commitment to quality, authenticity, and culinary exploration, the menu at Cucina Torcicoda presents a diverse range of dishes to satisfy discerning palates.

Sabatini

Address: Via Panzani, 9A

Phone: +39 055 282802

Designed by architect Stigler in 1955, Sabatini offers a unique ambiance with its furnishings sourced from a deconsecrated 16th-century church. Recognized as a cultural heritage site by the Fine Arts, the restaurant preserves cherished memories left by the artists and aristocrats who frequented it in the 1970s. The spacious interior includes the Giardino d'Inverno, the largest and most expansive room within the establishment. Sabatini takes pride in serving high-quality classic Tuscan cuisine, reinterpreting ancient Florentine recipes with a modern touch. Indulge in elegant and refined dishes that harmoniously blend taste, quality, and simplicity, including the must-try Florentine steak, grilled specialties, and fresh pasta creations.

Atelier De' Nerli

Address: Piazza De' Nerli, 9r

Phone: +39 338 5988273

Atelier De' Nerli, conceived by the creative mind of Daniele Cavalli, is a fusion of art, craftsmanship, and culinary excellence. This remarkable establishment seamlessly combines a gastronomic experience rooted in Tuscan traditions with a profound appreciation for artisanal craftsmanship and the spirit of contemporary artists such as painters, photographers, and sculptors. The restaurant proudly showcases and offers for sale the works of these talented individuals. Embracing the ethos of a true artisanal workshop, Atelier De' Nerli captivates diners with dishes like sautéed scallops in butter with chili-infused artichokes and filet with three peppers accompanied by Worcestershire cream and Dijon mustard.

Saporium Firenze

Address: Lungarno Benvenuto Cellini, 69r

Phone: +39 055 212933

Nestled along Lungarno Cellini, Saporium Firenze occupies the esteemed location once held by La Bottega del Buon Caffè, bringing the philosophy and haute cuisine of Borgo Santo Pietro in Chiusdino to the heart of Florence. Under the guidance of Executive Chef Ariel Hagen and his talented team, guests embark on a sensory journey inspired by Borgo Santo Pietro's farm-to-table concept. Saporium Firenze offers three distinctive tasting menus: Territorial Projections, Pes-care, and Vegetable Depths, showcasing Chef Ariel's exceptional dishes that have already gained acclaim at Borgo Santo Pietro. Additionally, the restaurant welcomes guests for lunch, presenting a slightly lighter three-course menu.

Georgia Tucker

Cantinetta Antinori

Address: Piazza Degli Antinori, 3

Phone: +39 055 292234

Since 1957, Cantinetta Antinori has stood as one of Florence's most renowned destinations for wine and cuisine. Situated in Piazza Antinori, adjacent to Via de' Tornabuoni, this esteemed restaurant occupies the ground floor of the prestigious Antinori building. Within an elegant and discreet environment, guests have the opportunity to savor an extensive selection of Antinori wines. Cantinetta Antinori's culinary offerings revolve around meticulously sourced and carefully selected ingredients, with a focus on seasonal and local products, predominantly from the Tuscan region. Delight in their enticing menu, featuring options such as cecina with squid and shrimp, ossobuco prepared in the Florentine style, and pappardelle with Tuscan ragout.

Cibreo Ristorante

Address: Via Del Verrocchio, 8r

Phone: +39 055 2341100

Led by the talented chef and kitchen maestro Fabio Picchi, Cibreo Ristorante holds a revered place in the heart of Florence, embodying an ancient Florentine tradition and an unwavering passion for authentic flavors. The seafood is sourced from the Tuscan sea, while the radicchio originates from the vegetable gardens tended by local farmers in the province of Florence. The cheeses come from nearby shepherds, and the oregano is exclusively procured from Francesca di Pantelleria, a trusted and long-standing supplier. Other notable ingredients include Sicilian lemons, San Miniato truffles, Calabrian clementines, and pasta from Puglia. Since 1979, Cibreo Ristorante has remained a refined fusion of flavors and fragrances, guided by the masterful touch of Chef Fabio Picchi. Noteworthy dishes include the yellow pepper purée, cod à la Cassi, stuffed neck, and Florentine stew.

Cibrèo Ristorante

Address: Via Dei Vecchietti, 5 50123 Florence - Italy

Phone: +39 055 2665651

The iconic Cibrèo extends its presence within the city center of Florence with the opening of a brand new Cibrèo Ristorante in the exclusive location of the historic Helvetia & Bristol Firenze – Starhotels Collezione. This new venture presents a fresh menu featuring meticulously selected Italian specialties. Among the must-try dishes are the Crespelle di Ricotta with White Meat Ragout, a symbol of Cibrèo's generous cuisine, and the Filetto di Fassona Piemontese, representing the pinnacle of quality and excellence in Italian ingredients. Another standout creation is L'Abetone, an elegantly asymmetrical dessert that playfully nods to the traditional Mont Blanc, encapsulating the Florentine flair synonymous with Cibrèo. Complementing the culinary experience is the newly introduced Cocktail Bar, offering a range of signature cocktails, classic international concoctions, and an extensive selection of spirits and liqueurs.

Se-Sto on Arno (Westin Excelsior)

Address: Piazza Ognissanti, 3

Phone: +39 055 27152783

Georgia Tucker

Perched on the sixth floor of The Westin Excelsior, Se-Sto on Arno boasts a futuristic architectural design characterized by uninterrupted glass windows, providing guests with breathtaking panoramic views of the city. For an extraordinary experience, consider reserving Table 41, which affords a mesmerizing vista of the Arno River with the Duomo as its backdrop. The exclusive menu at Se-Sto on Arno features a range of tantalizing dishes, including Tagliatella with rabbit and rosemary, leek cream and black truffle, as well as braised pork cheek accompanied by soft polenta bramata. With a maximum capacity of 80 seats, the restaurant welcomes guests from 12 pm to 10 pm.

Harry's Bar

Address: Lungarno Vespucci, 22r

Phone: +39 055 2396700

For over 50 years, Harry's Bar has played host to a multitude of notable personalities, including Paloma Picasso, Burt Lancaster, Margot Hemingway, Paul Newman, Robin Williams, Franco Zeffirelli, Elizabeth Taylor, and Chelsea Clinton. Situated along Lungarno Vespucci, the restaurant offers an outdoor dehor that provides a splendid view of the Lungarno. Impeccable service accompanies a menu featuring unforgettable dishes, such as Taglierini au gratin à la Harry's Bar, shrimp tails with curry, and beef tartare. Vegetarian and gluten-free options are also available for lunch throughout the week. And before departing, be sure to savor the historic Bellini cocktail.

Harry's Bar The Garden

Address: Via Il Prato 42

Phone: +39 055 277 1704

Harry's Bar The Garden seamlessly embraces the exclusive atmosphere of Sina Villa Medici, creating an enchanting dining experience underscored by traditional cuisine and meticulous attention to detail. The extraordinary location, complemented by soft lighting and a picturesque view of the garden with its swimming pool, adds an element of magic and creates indelible memories for guests.

Ora d'Aria

Via Dei Georgofili, 11r

Phone: +39 055 2001699

Ora d'Aria is a prominent establishment in Florentine haute cuisine, offering two tasting menus and an à la carte option. The culinary creations of Chef Marco Stabile take center stage, featuring dishes that showcase the artistry of eggs, traditional family recipes, risotto, guinea fowl, roasted pigeon etouffè with apple and puntarelle, and venison steak. Chef Stabile's remarkable talent shines through, delivering surprising flavors and a constant pursuit of culinary excellence.

Osteria delle Tre Panche - Hotel Hermitage

Vicolo Marzio, 1

Phone: +39 055 583724

Georgia Tucker

Osteria delle Tre Panche presents a delightful culinary journey infused with truffle flavors. With its picturesque location overlooking the Ponte Vecchio and a sixth-floor terrace offering panoramic views of the city's iconic landmarks, this dining experience is truly unforgettable. The menu offers a range of delectable dishes inspired by Tuscan and Italian traditions. Immerse yourself in the magic of Florence as you savor the flavors of Osteria delle Tre Panche and feel as though you can almost reach out and touch Ponte Vecchio.

Palazzo Portinari Salviati

Via del Corso, 6

Phone: +39 055 535 3555

Palazzo Portinari-Salviati welcomes guests to the new hospitality and food and wine project led by Vito Mollica. Within this historical setting, the Bistrot invites visitors to indulge in an "All Day Menu" featuring culinary offerings inspired by Tuscan and Italian traditions. The Cocktail Bar offers an intimate ambiance dedicated to signature mixology. For small events, Sala Beatrice provides a private room with a convivial table, accommodating up to 40 guests. Finally, the gastronomic restaurant Chic Nonna, located in the oldest part of Palazzo Portinari Salviati, showcases a seasonal menu with a traditional foundation and an international twist.

Golden View

Via de Bardi 58r

Phone: +39 055 214502

The Golden View celebrates an important milestone, its twentieth anniversary, as a destination that combines culinary pleasures with breathtaking views. Founded by Tommaso Grasso, the Golden View has become a haven for those seeking both exceptional dining experiences and picturesque surroundings. Chef Paolo Secci presents a menu that highlights the gastronomic excellence of the Tuscan region, complemented by a carefully curated wine selection managed by wine manager Paolo Milano. From the restaurant's windows, guests can admire the vibrant fish market with an abundance of Mediterranean delicacies, including Sicilian specialties like tuna, swordfish, Mazara red prawns, purple shrimp, and more.

Georgia Tucker

CHAPTER FIVE

TOP-RATED TOURIST ATTRACTIONS IN FLORENCE, ITALY

Florence boasts an array of captivating attractions that could occupy weeks of exploration. Each of its numerous churches could easily serve as the main tourist draw for a smaller city, while iconic landmarks such as Ponte Vecchio, Michelangelo's David, and Brunelleschi's Dome have become renowned symbols of Italy's rich cultural heritage. This city is a living testament to the Italian Renaissance, an artistic movement that revolutionized Europe after the Dark Ages.

Amidst this impressive collection of palaces, churches, museums, and landmarks, certain attractions stand out for their exceptional significance. As you plan your sightseeing itinerary in Florence, it is essential to prioritize these highlights, which have contributed to the city's status as one of Europe's most popular destinations. To ensure you experience the best that Florence has to offer, refer to this comprehensive list of top-rated attractions and activities.

1. Cathedral Of Santa Maria Del Fiore And Piazza Duomo

Piazza Duomo and its cathedral complex bring together some of Italy's most treasured artistic wonders within a relatively compact area. Exploring the baptistery, bell tower, cathedral, and museum, visitors encounter masterpieces by revered artists of the Italian Renaissance, including Ghiberti, Brunelleschi,

Georgia Tucker

Donatello, Giotto, and Michelangelo.

Begin by strolling around the square to marvel at the intricate marble facades before venturing inside each structure to appreciate the mesmerizing stained-glass artwork that greets you at every turn.

To avoid long queues, especially on hot days, consider the Skip the Line: Florence Duomo with Brunelleschi's Dome Climb tour. This 2.5-hour guided experience encompasses the cathedral, dome, and baptistery, offering entrance fees and the opportunity to independently explore the Opera del Duomo Museum.

2. Battistero Di San Giovanni (Baptistery Of St. John)

From any perspective, both inside and outside, the 12th-century octagonal baptistery showcases unparalleled artistry. Its marble facade, intricate interior mosaics, and the remarkable works of art it houses all deserve a prominent place on your itinerary.

However, the crowning glory is undoubtedly the magnificent bronze panels adorning the doors facing the cathedral. Known as the Gates of Paradise, these panels crafted by Ghiberti exemplify bronze craftsmanship at its finest. For a closer look at these extraordinary creations and other treasures associated with the baptistery, a visit to the Museo dell'Opera del Duomo, the cathedral's museum, is highly recommended.

3. See Florence From Piazzale Michelangiolo

Piazzale Michelangelo, often mistakenly referred to as Piazzale Michelangelo, is an iconic terrace above the city that holds significant appeal for tourists. It is a popular stop for tour buses, offering the perfect vantage point for capturing postcard-worthy photographs of the cathedral. To enjoy a more tranquil experience, it is advisable to visit during the late afternoon or early evening, particularly at sunset.

While the dome of the cathedral provides a 360-degree panorama of Florence, it is only from Piazzale Michelangelo that one can fully grasp the commanding presence of Brunelleschi's dome over the city center. This terrace also offers a sweeping view of renowned landmarks such as Ponte Vecchio, Palazzo Vecchio, and Santa Croce, providing a unique perspective of Florence's architectural splendor.

Reaching Piazzale Michelangelo can be done by taking a leisurely walk through the gardens from the riverbank or by utilizing bus routes 12 or 13. For an extended exploration, visitors can continue their journey up to the church of San Miniato al Monte or return downhill on the bus after visiting the church.

4. Uffizi Palace And Gallery

The Uffizi Palace stands indisputably among the world's most esteemed art museums, captivating visitors with its extraordinary collection. The sheer diversity and quality of the artworks housed within its walls are awe-inspiring, even to those with a limited interest in art. It is essential to witness the highlights of the paintings showcased here.

A visit to the Uffizi allows a deeper understanding of how Florentine painters from the 14th to 16th centuries revolutionized Western art. The transition from Byzantine-style images to lifelike depictions of figures and landscapes by Renaissance artists is particularly evident within this collection.

Originally one of the palaces belonging to the Medici family, the Uffizi Palace was purposefully designed not as a residence but as a multifunctional space for governmental offices, scientific studies, and the expanding art collection. Notably, the exquisite octagonal Tribuna was commissioned specifically to exhibit the most treasured paintings and jewels of Francesco I de' Medici.

To bypass the long queues for admission, visitors can opt for a Skip the Line: Florence Accademia and Uffizi Gallery Tour, which offers priority access and a guided tour.

5. Piazza Della Signoria And The Loggia Dei Lanzi

Dating back to the 14th century, Piazza della Signoria has served as the epicenter of power in Florence and is believed to have historical roots that trace even further back to Etruscan and Roman civilizations. Today, it remains a vibrant social hub, attracting both tourists and locals alike. The focal point of the square is the Neptune Fountain, while the Palazzo Vecchio, which still houses the city's government, stands proudly on one side.

Adjacent to the Uffizi Palace, forming one end of the piazza, is the Loggia dei Lanzi—an open-air sculpture gallery featuring several remarkable pieces. Among them, Benvenuto Cellini's renowned work, "Perseus with the Head of Medusa," is widely recognized. Additionally, a replica of Michelangelo's "David" stands before the Palazzo Vecchio, adding to the artistic allure of the square.

6. Galleria Dell'accademia (Academy Gallery)

Within the walls of this art museum lies Michelangelo's most celebrated masterpiece, the original "David." Although the sculpture is now protected behind glass due to a previous incident, it still exudes an inspirational aura that never fails to captivate viewers.

The Academy Gallery not only houses the iconic "David" but also displays other noteworthy works by Michelangelo. Observing the four unfinished slaves within the same gallery provides a glimpse into Michelangelo's artistic process, as these sculptures, originally intended for a Roman tomb, seem to emerge gradually from the marble.

Additionally, the gallery features Michelangelo's unfinished "St. Matthew" intended for Florence Cathedral, along with captivating highlights by Florentine artists from the 13th to 16th centuries. Noteworthy among them is Sandro Botticelli's striking Madonna.

Georgia Tucker

To save time and avoid long queues at both the Academy Gallery and Uffizi, visitors can take advantage of a Skip the Line: Florence Accademia and Uffizi Gallery Tour, providing direct access and a guided tour.

7. San Lorenzo And Michelangelo's Medici Tombs

San Lorenzo showcases the Medici family's commitment to commissioning exceptional talent for their family church and burial chapels. Brunelleschi was entrusted with the construction of the church, while Michelangelo was tasked with creating the chapel intended to honor the Medici's most illustrious members. Although both artists passed away before completing their respective works, Brunelleschi's church was finished according to his original plans.

Michelangelo's chapel, known as the New Sacristy, remains an unfinished masterpiece, yet its sculptural achievements in marble are considered among the finest in the world. Exploring the church, the Old Sacristy, the New Sacristy, the Princes' Chapel, and the Laurenziana Library provides an opportunity to encounter additional works by Renaissance masters, including Donatello and Lippi.

8. Palazzo Vecchio (Palazzo Della Signoria)

A bastion of history, art, and power, Palazzo Vecchio stands as a fortress-like palace in the heart of Florence. This magnificent structure served as the ruling center of the city and the Republic of Florence, with the powerful Medici family enlisting the most accomplished artists and architects of their time to design and embellish their offices and residences.

It is advisable to sign up early for one of the complimentary tours to explore the opulent rooms and grand galleries, granting access to secret passages used by the Medici to navigate between chambers. Additionally, returning in the evening (while retaining the ticket) allows visitors to ascend to the roof and witness breathtaking sunset views of the city.

9. Santa Croce

Santa Croce is a remarkable church and mausoleum that pays tribute to some of Florence's most revered figures, while also boasting an impressive collection of Renaissance art. Noteworthy highlights within this iconic site include the Cappella Bardi, adorned with major frescoes by Giotto, and the adjacent Cappella Peruzzi, which inspired the artistic endeavors of Masaccio and Michelangelo. Additionally, Donatello's Christ Crucified stands as a remarkable embodiment of Florentine Renaissance humanism.

Georgia Tucker

The frescoes within the Cappella Baroncelli, masterfully crafted by Taddeo Gaddi, are regarded as his greatest achievement. However, the pinnacle of Santa Croce's artistic splendor is Cimabue's magnificent Crucifix, heralded for its pioneering transition from rigid Byzantine aesthetics to the naturalistic style of the Renaissance, which profoundly influenced subsequent artistic luminaries. As you explore the nave, you will encounter the final resting places of esteemed individuals such as Michelangelo, Galileo, Ghiberti, the renowned composer Gioacchino Rossini, and even Machiavelli.

10. Ponte Vecchio

Undoubtedly the most recognizable symbol of Florence, the Ponte Vecchio enchants visitors with its graceful arches and the charming assortment of shops that adorns its structure. Historically, this bridge served as a haven for the city's skilled goldsmiths, and to this day, a stroll across it reveals a dazzling array of exquisite jewelry. However, many tourists are unaware of the hidden treasures that lie above their heads. Originally designed to connect the two sides of the Arno River, the Medici family commissioned the architect Vasari to construct a passageway known as the Percorso del Principe or Vasari Corridor. Above the shops, you can observe a series of evenly spaced windows that form this passage. Yet, it is more than a mere corridor; its walls house a priceless collection of portraits, predominantly self-portraits, by esteemed artists such as Rembrandt, Leonardo da Vinci, Raphael, Michelangelo, and Velázquez.

11. Palazzo Pitti (Pitti Palace)

A visit to the Pitti Palace complex offers a captivating glimpse into the multifaceted allure of Florence. With its exceptional art gallery, Medici palace, representation of Florentine craftsmanship, museums, historical significance, royal apartments, and magnificent gardens, the palace presents a microcosm of the city's diverse attractions. If time permits, a full day devoted to exploring the complex is highly rewarding. Alternatively, a tour of the palace enables you to marvel at the opulent Royal Apartments and the sumptuous rooms that showcase masterpieces by renowned artists such as Raphael, Titian, Rubens, Tintoretto, and others. Rather than being displayed in a traditional gallery format, these paintings adorn rooms specifically designed for entertainment and aesthetic pleasure, creating an immersive experience that rivals the renowned Uffizi Gallery.

12. Santa Maria Novella

Santa Maria Novella, a Dominican church, presents a distinct interpretation of the characteristic striped marble façade found in several other Florentine churches. Here, the façade features graceful curving designs that emulate windows, accentuating the rows of arches on the lower level. The artistic splendor continues within, showcasing some of the city's finest frescoes by esteemed masters such as Masaccio, Giotto, Domenico Ghirlandaio, Lippi, and Paolo Uccello. Moreover, an entire chapel is adorned with extraordinary frescoes by Andrea di Bonaiuto, representing some of the most exceptional artworks of 14th-century Italy. Alongside the frescoes, notable highlights include Brunelleschi's marble pulpit, his wooden crucifix, Vasari's Rosary Madonna, and a bronze sculpture by Lorenzo Ghiberti. Don't miss the opportunity to visit the historic pharmacy located within the convent, where herbal balms and floral lotions are available for purchase.

13. San Miniato Al Monte

The sight of San Miniato al Monte, with its stunning façade adorned with green-and-white inlaid marble, is a reward in itself, well worth the short climb beyond the renowned viewpoint of Florence, Piazzale Michelangiolo (or a brief bus ride away). The church's striking façade, among the first to exhibit this dramatic design in Florence, features a large gold mosaic at its pinnacle. Its portico design draws inspiration from Classical Roman architecture, while the Byzantine-inspired mosaics on the façade blend harmoniously with the new Tuscan Romanesque architectural style. Stepping inside, you'll find a spacious open nave with a mosaic floor and a painted wooden ceiling that culminates in a magnificent Renaissance chapel graced with a glazed blue-and-white terracotta ceiling. Further highlights include additional Byzantine-style mosaics, a 12th-century marble pulpit, and a beautifully decorated choir screen. Notably, the sacristy stands out as a truly remarkable space, adorned with vibrant panels from Spinello Aretino's 14th-century masterpiece, the Life of St. Benedict. This sacristy ranks among Florence's most splendid rooms, on par with those found in the grandest palaces.

Address: Via delle Porte Sante, 34, Florence

14. Bargello Palace National Museum

The Bargello Palace is a must-visit destination in Florence, particularly due to the presence of four exceptional masterpieces by Michelangelo. Moreover, the palace showcases work by renowned artists such as Donatello, the della Robbias, Cellini, Brunelleschi, Ghiberti, and Tuscan artists from the 14th to the 16th century. The palace also houses a room dedicated to ivory carvings and a remarkable collection of majolica.

Of particular note is the palace's emphasis on decorative arts and sculpture, setting it apart from other art museums in Florence. Visitors will find an entire room devoted to enamels and goldwork, a distinct Florentine specialty during the Renaissance. This unique focus adds to the allure of the Bargello Palace as a cultural destination.

Address: Via del Proconsolo 4, Florence

15. Stroll Through Boboli Gardens

Situated behind the Pitti Palace, the Boboli Gardens were meticulously crafted by Grand Duke Cosimo I between 1550 and 1560, spanning an impressive 111 acres of green terraces. This grand endeavor served as a model for royal gardens throughout Europe, including the renowned Gardens of Versailles. The gardens' beautifully maintained landscape gradually ascends, offering panoramic views of the city from various overlooks.

Within the gardens, visitors will encounter an array of captivating features, including fountains, statuary, and the Grotta del Buontalenti—a simulated cave with intricately carved stalactites and stalagmites. Other notable attractions include a maze, formal flower beds, and an amphitheater located in a quarry hole that resulted from stone extraction for the palace's construction. At the highest point of the gardens stands the terrace of the Kaffeehaus, while the Casino del Cavaliere, overlooking the Boboli Gardens, houses a rich collection of porcelain owned by ruling families, including the Medici and the Savoy.

16. Explore The Oltrarno And Take A Break In Piazza Santo Spirito

The Oltrarno neighborhood offers a delightful exploration of atmospheric lanes brimming with workshops and studios of Florence's esteemed artists specializing in woodwork, silver and gold craftsmanship, gilding, miniature mosaics, decorative papers, and leather bookbinding. These artisanal workshops offer a tempting array of finely crafted items for sale, making them ideal for finding exquisite souvenirs or gifts like beautifully bound journals or gilded wooden boxes.

A visit to Piazza Santo Spirito is highly recommended, as this lively square exudes an intimate ambiance distinct from the grander and busier squares across the river. Taking a seat at an outdoor table in one of the cafes or restaurants allows visitors to observe the bustling morning market or enjoy the sight of children playing ball after school.

Although the Basilica of Santo Spirito may not be as well-known as other churches in Florence, it stands as a pure Renaissance masterpiece, adorned with notable paintings and sculptures, particularly within the transept chapels.

17. Palazzo Medici-Riccardi

Palazzo Medici-Riccardi, completed in 1464, offers more restrained furnishing and decor compared to the ostentatious palaces associated with later generations of the Medici family. The palace aligns with the earlier dukes who governed during a more democratic era in Florentine society. For almost a century, it served as the residence of the Medicis until Cosimo I relocated to the Palazzo Vecchio.

Ascending the staircase from the courtyard leads visitors to the Palace Chapel, adorned with well-preserved frescoes by Benozzo Gozzoli, providing a vivid glimpse into court life during 15th-century Florence. While subsequent alterations were made by the Riccardi family, who owned the palace after the Medicis, the Medici Museum on the ground floor retains the original Medici interior. Noteworthy among the museum's treasures is Filippo Lippi's significant work, Madonna and Child, painted in 1442.

Address: Via Cavour 1 & 3, Florence

Official site: www.palazzo-medici.it

18. Mercato Centrale: Florence's Food Market

If one starts to perceive Florence as merely a vast open-air museum, a visit to Mercato Centrale provides a chance to encounter the city's inhabitants as they go about their daily routines. This expansive food market offers an authentic glimpse into local life, with its bustling atmosphere and a cornucopia of enticing aromas emanating from fresh herbs, flowers, and garden produce. Amidst the crowd, one can mingle with locals, particularly women gathering ingredients for their evening meals.

The market also serves as an excellent source for delightful gifts to bring back home, including fine Tuscan olive oils, olives, candied fruits, and delectable nougat. On the upper floor, visitors will find food courts, providing a convenient spot for a quick lunch.

Address: Piazza del Mercato, Florence

19. Bardini Museum And Gardens

Artist and collector Stefano Bardini acquired several buildings on a hillside in the Oltrarno district overlooking Florence in the late 19th century. From these structures, which included a chapel and a former 14th-century palazzo, Bardini fashioned a setting for his extensive collections of art and priceless antiquities.

To create this unique museum, Bardini incorporated architectural elements salvaged from demolished medieval and Renaissance buildings. The resulting palazzo houses magnificent artworks alongside these architectural features, presenting visitors with an eccentric yet captivating environment. Additionally, Bardini purchased a neighboring garden overlooking the river, transforming it into an outdoor gallery to exhibit his sculpture collections.

The Bardini Gardens, overlooking Florence, provide a serene escape from the bustling crowds, offering a tranquil haven amidst greenery and blossoms. April is a particularly enchanting time to visit, as vibrant purple wisteria envelops the pergola and perfumes the air. A grand staircase, mosaic fountains, an English garden, and a terrace with a café further enhance the garden's appeal. The entrance to the garden is separate from the museum.

20. Brancacci Chapel

Despite its unassuming façade, Santa Maria del Carmine church houses one of the greatest masterpieces of the 15th century within its walls. The chapel's frescoes, created by renowned artists Masaccio and Masolino in the early 1400s, depict scenes from the life of St. Peter and the Old Testament. These works of art demonstrate the remarkable vibrancy and utilize perspective techniques, showcasing Masaccio's pioneering use of perspective and his ability to infuse his figures with lifelike expressions and energy.

Masaccio considered the leading Italian painter of the Quattrocento period and a pioneer of the Early Italian Renaissance, left the chapel unfinished. Filippino Lippi later completed the remaining portions in the late 1400s. Despite its significance as a landmark and its status as a magnificent work of art, the Brancacci Chapel remains one of Florence's lesser-known treasures.

Address: Piazza del Carmine 14, Florence

21. Museo Galileo

Amidst Florence's rich collection of Renaissance art encompassing painting, sculpture, and architecture, it is essential not to overlook the profound scientific advancements that shaped this transformative era. The Humanists, seeking liberation from religious constraints, embraced the exploration of the universe, recognizing the inseparable bond between art and science.

The Museo Galileo exemplifies this interconnection, housing an extraordinary array of astronomical, navigational, surveying, and exploratory instruments that transcend their utilitarian purpose and assume the status of priceless works of art. Within its collections of compasses, tools, and magnificent world globes, visitors can marvel at Galileo's instruments alongside masterful creations by Florence's foremost artists, crafted from metals, wood, gold, and other artistic mediums.

Address: Piazza dei Giudici 1, Florence

Official site: https://www.museogalileo.it/en/

22. Shop For Leather At Piazza Santa Croce

Florence has a longstanding tradition of fine leather craftsmanship, dating back to the Renaissance era when leatherworkers established their workshops near Santa Croce, close to the riverside tanneries. To procure the highest quality leather goods at fair prices, the neighborhood surrounding Santa Croce remains the premier destination. It is advisable to explore the leatherwork school or artisan studio shops, as certain establishments, such as street market vendors, offer imported and imitation leather products.

Within the cloister of Santa Croce, the Scuola di Cuoio leatherworking school showcases exceptional handcrafted leather items, affording visitors the opportunity to observe students fashioning wallets, boxes, handbags, and leather jackets. Notably, Francesca Gori's exclusive handbags, crafted from rare and exotic leathers and specifically designed for the school, can be found here. Additionally, the school presents an assortment of luggage, bound books, belts, jewelry boxes, and leather garments. Adjacent to Piazza Santa Croce, Misuri occupies a former palazzo adorned with frescoes, showcasing equally remarkable traditional craftsmanship and designs.

Address: Piazza Santa Croce, Florence

Official site: www.scuoladelcuoio.com

Georgia Tucker

CHAPTER SIX

21 BEST MUSEUMS IN FLORENCE

Florence, the cultural and historical hub of Tuscany in Italy, captivates visitors with its abundance of art, culture, and heritage. Known as the "Jewel of the Renaissance," the city's historic center, a UNESCO World Heritage Site, attracts millions of tourists annually, eager to immerse themselves in the city's extraordinary art and architecture. Florence pulsates with creativity and inspiration, evident at every turn, whether it be marveling at the Duomo, enjoying an espresso in a 16th-century frescoed building, or strolling through majestic palaces and enchanting gardens.

Exploring the museums in Florence is an essential part of any visit. Bursting with vibrant colors, intricate details, and historical significance, each museum offers a fascinating journey. From renowned art galleries like the Uffizi Gallery, one of the oldest and most celebrated in the world, and the Accademia Gallery, home to Michelangelo's iconic statue of David, to historical institutions such as the Archaeological Museum, there is something to captivate every visitor. Moreover, Florence is replete with smaller museums, palaces, monasteries, and aristocratic residences that hide remarkable treasures, waiting to be discovered.

From world-renowned art collections and historic residences to quirky science museums and hidden gems, Florence's museums cater to diverse interests and budgets. Without further delay, let us delve into the finest museums Florence has to offer.

1 – Uffizi Gallery

Situated just a short stroll from the iconic Ponte Vecchio, the Uffizi Gallery entices art enthusiasts like a beacon, drawing over two million visitors annually. This prestigious museum, one of the world's oldest and most renowned, houses a rich and diverse collection spanning from ancient sculptures to masterpieces of the Middle Ages and the modern era. Its hallowed halls showcase works by legendary artists, including Leonardo da Vinci, Michelangelo, Simone Martini, Piero della Francesca, Beato Angelico, Filippo Lippi, Botticelli, Mantegna, Giotto, Cimabue, Raffaello (Raphael), Caravaggio, and many others. The gallery also features European artworks by German, Dutch, and Finnish artists.

Georgia Tucker

Originally commissioned by Cosimo I de Medici, the first Grand Duke of Tuscany, in 1560 as government offices (hence the name "Uffizi," meaning "offices"), the building's transformation into a public art museum occurred in 1765. Its historical significance and architectural splendor mirror the artistic treasures displayed within. While visitors can explore the majestic halls at their own pace with a general admission ticket (20 euros for adults, free for children under 18), a guided tour is highly recommended. Led by knowledgeable art experts, these tours offer a comprehensive exploration of each painting, shedding light on the artist, the historical context, and cultural significance.

For a deeper understanding, the self-guided audio tour (available in Italian, English, French, Spanish, German, Polish, Russian, and Japanese) provides fascinating insights, immersing visitors in the intricacies of the artworks. If you plan to visit multiple museums in Florence, the Passepartout 5 Days ticket (38 euros) offers exceptional value, granting access to the Uffizi Gallery, Pitti

Palace, and the Boboli Gardens for five consecutive days. The Uffizi Gallery opens from Tuesday to Sunday, 8:15 am to 6:30 pm, and features a charming cafe and a bookstore filled with delightful souvenirs.

2 – Museo di Palazzo Vecchio

Originally designed as the seat of the city's government, the Palazzo Vecchio evolved into the residence of the Medici family, who ruled Florence during most of the 15th through 18th centuries. This iconic medieval palace, an emblem of Florence's illustrious past, commands attention with its imposing presence atop the Piazza della Signoria. Yet, it offers far more than architectural grandeur.

Within its walls, visitors can explore a labyrinth of secret passages, marvel at frescoed ceilings, and admire well-preserved artworks. The palace vividly narrates the story of bygone eras and provides insights into the city's transformation under the rule of powerful families like the Medici dynasty. The Palazzo Vecchio seamlessly merges art and history, making it a must-visit for those intrigued by Florence's complex past and eager to witness celebrated paintings and decorations up close.

The museum's admission fee (12.5 euros for adults, free for children under 17) makes it an accessible destination, allowing ample time to explore its opulent rooms for 2-3 hours. Opting for a guided tour offers a curated experience, ensuring that visitors don't miss the highlights. Notably, the Hall of 500 stands out as the most impressive space within the palace. For panoramic views of Florence, daring visitors can climb the 233 steps to the top of the 95-meter-tall bell tower, the oldest section of the structure dating back over seven centuries (beware if you have a fear of heights!).

Located a short walk from the Uffizi Gallery, the Palazzo Vecchio Museum welcomes visitors every day except Thursday from 9 am to 7 pm (closing at 2 pm on Thursdays). The Palazzo itself remains open until 10 pm, allowing for leisurely exploration.

3 – Museo Dell'opera Di Santa Maria Del Fiore

Established in 1296 to house the commissioned artworks for the construction of Florence Cathedral, the Museo dell'Opera di Santa Maria del Fiore, also known as the Florence Cathedral Museum, stands as one of Europe's oldest museums and a custodian of Italy's most renowned sculptures and artworks.

A must-visit for devoted art enthusiasts, this remarkable museum offers a captivating journey through time, commencing with the original plans and models of the iconic cathedral, completed circa 1367, before delving into the artistic treasures adorning its exterior.

Within its walls reside a myriad of captivating sculptures, intricate drawings, and paintings, created by some of the world's most celebrated artists. Among the notable highlights, Ghiberti's bronze baptistery doors, Donatello's carved wooden depiction of Mary Magdalene, and Michelangelo's evocative Pietà stand out, accompanied by other masterpieces crafted by revered artists such as Andrea Pisano and Luca della Robbia. Noteworthy is the wooden and brick model, conceived by Brunelleschi, the architect of the Duomo, with assistance from Donatello and Nanni di Banco, showcasing the visionary plans for the emblematic cathedral.

While admission to the museum is included in the Brunelleschi, Giotto, and Ghiberti packages, which offer different combinations of attractions in the vicinity, individual access to the museum is priced at 18 euros. It's important to note that if you opt solely to visit the cathedral and not the museum, there is no charge.

Worth mentioning is the museum's top floor, featuring a specially designed study room catering to the visually impaired. Here, visitors have the opportunity to interact with reproductions of artworks and models displayed throughout the museum, exemplifying a commendable commitment to inclusivity that sets it apart from many other institutions.

Georgia Tucker

4 – Accademia Gallery

Situated in the heart of the Renaissance birthplace, the Accademia Gallery is hailed as one of Florence's premier museums, renowned for its diverse collection of Renaissance paintings and sculptures.

However, the museum's most iconic masterpiece is undoubtedly Michelangelo's David, an unparalleled artistic treasure of monumental proportions that has garnered worldwide acclaim.

This larger-than-life marble sculpture, created between 1501 and 1504 to depict the biblical hero before slaying Goliath, stands as a testament to the strength and youthful beauty. Its awe-inspiring presence, standing at a towering 14 feet, mesmerizes viewers with its immaculate craftsmanship. While it is tempting to devote all attention to this extraordinary piece, it is highly recommended to explore the entirety of the museum's collection.

Within the gallery's halls, visitors will encounter several other works by Michelangelo, including four unfinished Prisoners or Slaves – The Awakening Slave, The Young Slave, The Bearded Slave, and The Atlas (or Bound) – housed in The Hall of Prisoners, originally intended for Pope Julius II's tomb.

However, the artistic richness is not limited to Michelangelo alone. As you wander through the adorned corridors and passageways, you will discover captivating paintings by Italian artists such as Botticelli, Lo Scheggia, Baldovinetti, and Pontormo, alongside an extensive collection of musical instruments from the Renaissance era.

Don't miss the Coronation of the Virgin panel painting by Jacopo Di Cione, as well as the Tree of Life by Pacino di Buonaguida.

The Accademia Gallery is open every day except Monday, operating from [opening time] to [closing time] (last entry at [last entry time]). For admission, the cost is 12 euros for adults, with an additional 4 euro booking fee, amounting to 16 euros. Discounts are available for students and EU residents, while children under 18 enjoy free entry. For optimal value, consider combining your visit with a city tour or a trip to the Uffizi Gallery.

A helpful tip: If you prefer spontaneous planning and potential cost savings, last-minute tickets for the Accademia Gallery can often be found online through various sources. Due to the museum's popularity, tickets may frequently be sold out at the official source. However, with the right knowledge, you can secure your visit seamlessly.

5 – Museo Archeologico Nazionale

Offering a refreshing departure from the abundance of Renaissance art scattered throughout Florence's many museums, the National Archaeological Museum stands as one of the city's largest and most significant institutions (distinct from the eponymous museum in Naples). Within its walls, an extraordinary collection of Etruscan, Egyptian, and Greek works, as well as a remarkable array of detailed and diverse Roman sculptures, awaits exploration.

Located near the Accademia Museum, the Archaeological Museum resides in the magnificent setting of Piazza della Santissima Annunziata, housed within an architectural gem that has come to be expected from Florence's grandeur. Its expansive garden features Etruscan tombs, providing an added dimension to the museum experience.

As you meander through the museum's halls, keep an eye out for several of its notable treasures. These include the sarcophagus of Laerthia Seianti from the 2nd century BC, an Egyptian war chariot, and the François vase dating back to 570 B.C. The Egyptian section, in particular, commands attention, as the museum proudly boasts the second-largest Egyptian collection in Italy, an astonishing feature that is sure to impress.

For those who revel in unearthing hidden gems and lesser-known works, take the time to appreciate the smaller objects on display throughout the museum. Among them are Roman mosaics, Greek vases, and a collection of amulets from antiquity. Don't miss the upstairs corridor, where you can admire a stunning selection of ancient gems from the Medici collections.

The National Archaeological Museum welcomes visitors from Tuesday to Friday, operating from 9 am to 8 pm, and from 9 am to 4 pm on weekends (closed on Mondays). Admission fees amount to 5 euros, with guided tours available for those seeking a more educational experience beyond mere browsing.

A helpful tip: Similar to acquiring tickets for the Accademia Gallery, last-minute tickets for the National Archaeological Museum can often be found online through various sources. To maximize your experience and value, consider purchasing the Uffizi Gallery 5 museum ticket, which grants you access to the Museo Archeologico Nazionale at no additional cost.

6 – La Specola – Natural History Museum

The Museo di Storia Naturale della Specola, located in Florence, is a remarkable museum that holds the distinction of being the oldest scientific museum in Europe. While it may not enjoy the same level of fame as renowned galleries like the Uffizi, Accademia, or Archaeological Museum, it is a hidden gem that should not be overlooked, particularly for those with an interest in the realms of science and nature.

One of the museum's most intriguing features is its collection of wax anatomical models, created in the 18th century by Gaetano Giulio Zumbo, an individual captivated by the intricacies of anatomy and corruption. These lifelike models offer a captivating and somewhat eerie glimpse into the state of medical science during that era. Be prepared for a striking departure from the conventional exhibits found at Madame Tussauds, as La Specola's nude wax figures, in provocative poses with exposed organs and open ribcages, present a distinct and haunting experience.

Georgia Tucker

The Museo di Storia Naturale della Specola, situated on Via Romana on the southern side of the Arno River, near the Pitti Palace, boasts a diverse array of attractions. Alongside the wax anatomical models, the museum showcases an extensive collection of minerals, including some of the world's largest crystals, meteorites, fossils, taxidermied animals, and an impressive Skeletons Hall on the ground floor. The museum also offers a dedicated section on archaic zoology, providing valuable insights into the evolution of various species throughout history. With over 3.5 million animals in its collection, approximately 5,000 of which are on display at any given time, there is much to explore and discover.

Beyond its captivating exhibits, the museum itself holds historical significance. Before the early 19th century, it stood as the only scientific museum in the world open to the public. For over two centuries, individuals seeking firsthand knowledge of natural history had to journey to Florence. Such a visit offered a unique and educational experience, reflective of a bygone era.

The Museo di Storia Naturale della Specola welcomes visitors from Tuesday to Sunday, operating from 10:30 am to 5:30 pm (closing an hour earlier from October 31 to May 31). The admission fee for adults is 6 euros, while children under 14 enter for 3 euros, and those under 6 can enjoy free entry. It is important to note that the anatomical collection is now accessible only through guided tours. Therefore, it is advisable to contact the museum in advance to reserve a spot or arrange a private group tour.

For those interested in immersing themselves in a full day of exploration, the nearby Boboli Gardens provide a tranquil and picturesque setting. With its Renaissance statues, ornate fountains, and expansive green spaces, the gardens offer a welcome respite and a delightful change of pace from the bustling Florentine museums.

7 – Museo Salvatore Ferragamo
The Museo Salvatore Ferragamo stands as a distinctive attraction in Florence, drawing fashion enthusiasts from around the world. Unlike traditional museums showcasing Renaissance paintings or marble sculptures, this museum focuses on the life and work of renowned Italian shoe designer Salvatore Ferragamo. Rising to fame during the 1920s in Hollywood, Ferragamo created iconic footwear for legendary celebrities such as Marilyn Monroe, Audrey Hepburn, and Greta Garbo. A visit to this museum provides a captivating glimpse into the fascinating realm of high fashion, Italian design, and Ferragamo's pivotal role in the history and development of footwear and international fashion.

Georgia Tucker

Housed within the grand Palazzo Spini Feroni on Via de' Tornabuoni, the Ferragamo museum occupies the basement of this historic building, constructed in 1289, which later became the company's headquarters and the first Salvatore Ferragamo store. The museum's vast collection spans three floors and encompasses over 14,000 items, including sketches, original prototypes, press cuttings, advertising materials, photographs, vintage shoes (dating back to the 1920s, with a collection of over 10,000 pairs), and films.

Among the numerous highlights are the shoes Ferragamo crafted for Hollywood celebrities like Judy Garland, Marilyn Monroe, Audrey Hepburn, and Sophia Loren. Ferragamo earned the title of "Shoemaker to the Stars" after establishing the 'Hollywood Boot Shop' in 1923. While the eccentric shoe collection showcases Ferragamo's craftsmanship and creativity, the museum also offers themed rotating exhibits that delve into broader topics such as silk or sustainability, offering visitors a comprehensive experience that extends beyond footwear.

The Ferragamo Museum welcomes visitors every day from 11 am to 7:30 pm. Admission for adults is 8 euros, with a 50% discount available for students and children. To enhance your visit, consider taking advantage of the free audio guides, offered in Italian, English, French, Spanish, and Japanese.

If you have a deep interest in fashion or desire to learn more about one of Florence's most illustrious sons, the Museo Salvatore Ferragamo is a must-visit. For those with an insatiable appetite for fashion, consider adding the Gucci Garden to your itinerary as well.

8 – Palatine Gallery at Palazzo Pitti

The Palatine Gallery, located within the Palazzo Pitti in Florence, stands as one of the most exquisite art museums in Italy, captivating visitors with its stunning and vibrant displays. Adorned with ornate gold trimmings on the ceilings and adorned with captivating artworks on the walls, the gallery offers an unparalleled visual feast.

Situated within the grand-ducal residence that was once home to the Medici and Lorraine families, the Pitti Palace, the Palatine Gallery occupies the entire first floor of the palace. The gallery was commissioned in 1458 by Luca Pitti, a Florentine banker and a friend of the Medici family. Its elongated and narrow layout was intended to serve as a venue for hosting grand events and displaying the remarkable art collection amassed by the Medici family.

The collection housed in the Palatine Gallery comprises works by renowned artists from the 16th and 17th centuries and beyond. Artists such as Titian, Rubens, Van Dyck, Raphael, Correggio, and Andrea del Sarto grace the walls with their masterpieces. Noteworthy pieces include Titian's Portrait of Vincenzo Mosti, Raphael's Portrait of Agnolo Doni and Ezekiel's Vision, and a wealth of other remarkable creations. The gallery's 28 rooms, many of which are named after planets or gods, feature high barrel-vaulted ceilings adorned with intricately detailed frescoes, adding to the overall splendor of the space.

The sheer abundance of masterpieces in such a confined area can be overwhelming for visitors attempting to absorb everything at once. The Palatine Gallery offers audio guides to assist in navigating and interpreting the artworks. These guides can prove invaluable in making sense of the collection's arrangement, which adheres to the same layout as during the Medici era and lacks a strict chronological order.

The Palatine Gallery is open every day except Mondays, operating from 1:30 pm to 6:30 pm. For a more serene experience, it is advisable to visit in the evening when the gallery tends to be less crowded than during the afternoon. Additionally, skip-the-line passes and private tours are available for those seeking a VIP experience. Admission for adults costs 23.75 euros, inclusive of a pre-sales fee of 4.75 euros (resulting in a net price of 19 euros). Discounts are offered to students and seniors. It is worth noting that the admission ticket also grants access to the Modern Art Gallery, the Costume Gallery, and the Medici Treasures, ensuring an enriching and comprehensive museum visit.

9 – Strozzi Palace

The Palazzo Strozzi, an impressive Renaissance palace, stands as an iconic landmark in Florence and serves as both a popular museum and a vibrant center for culture. Once the residence of the influential Strozzi banking family, this monumental palace now houses multiple cultural institutions and exhibitions, offering a comprehensive experience of Florentine art and culture. Notably, it features an exceptional temporary exhibition space that showcases a diverse range of artwork, including contemporary art, digital art, retrospectives, and medieval and Renaissance collections.

In addition to the exhibitions, visitors can explore a captivating medieval courtyard and a well-curated museum on the ground floor dedicated to the Strozzi family. The Palazzo Strozzi welcomes visitors daily from 10 am to 8 pm, with extended hours until 11 pm on Thursdays. Admission for adults is 15 euros, with discounted rates available for students, seniors, and free entry for children under 6. Enhancing the art experience, an audio guide is recommended, available in Italian and English for an additional fee, or alternatively, visitors can opt for a docent-led tour. Conveniently located near the Arno River, the Palazzo Strozzi offers splendid views from multiple angles and easy access to charming cafes and restaurants for post-visit refreshments.

10 – Bargello Museum

Nestled within the Palazzo del Bargello, formerly a fortress and prison transformed into an art museum, the Bargello Museum is

Georgia Tucker

widely recognized as Florence's foremost collection of historical artwork, second only to the Uffizi Gallery. Distinguished by its towering 54-meter clock tower, this museum, also known as the National Museum or National Bargello Museum, showcases an impressive and diverse assortment of sculptures spanning three floors. These include early examples of Renaissance art crafted by renowned artists such as Ghiberti, Brunelleschi, and Donatello, the latter two having made significant contributions to Florence's Duomo. Complementing the sculpture display are over 2500 paintings, forming a remarkable ensemble. Notable highlights feature Michelangelo's Bacchus, a life-size marble sculpture depicting the Greek and Roman god of wine, created when the artist was just 21 years old in 1497. The museum also boasts an array of notable works by Pisano, Verrocchio, Luca della Robbia, and Andrea Pisano, as well as a significant collection of medieval art, ivory artifacts, arms and armor, ceramics, waxes, enamels, medals, jewelry, tapestries, and the only bust ever created by Michelangelo, the Bust of Brutus. A must-visit is the Salone del Camino, a highly frequented room on the second floor, featuring meticulously crafted bronze statues by renowned artists such as Giambologna and Cellini. Due to its cultural significance, the Bargello Museum attracts considerable interest, especially since it closes in the early afternoon at 1:30 pm, prior to many other institutions. To avoid long queues and crowds, it is advisable to visit in the morning when it opens at 8:45 am. Adult tickets are priced at 8 euros, with free admission for children under 17. For an enriched experience, an audio guide is available in English, French, German, Italian, and Spanish for an additional fee of 6 euros.

11 – Stibbert Museum

Stepping into the Stibbert Museum feels akin to traveling back in time to the medieval era, immersing visitors in Florence's aristocratic past. This remarkable museum, conceived by art collector Frederick Stibbert, an eccentric English expatriate who inherited a substantial fortune, showcases his impressive collection of art and artifacts in a grand 19th-century villa, now incorporated into the city of Florence.

The museum's extensive holdings encompass over 36,000 items spanning Egyptian antiquities, Etruscan treasures, medieval armor and weapons, paintings, and tapestries. Stibbert's passion for weaponry is evident through the collection of over 16,000 European, Oriental, Islamic, and Japanese arms and armor, representing various historical periods from the 15th to the 19th century. Noteworthy among the displays is the magnificent Cavalcade Room, featuring over a dozen 16th-century knights on horseback, armor-clad foot soldiers, an abundance of swords, and an impressive assembly of 80 samurai suits. The museum also dedicates several rooms to Oriental artifacts, showcasing Stibbert's fascination with both Far Eastern and Western cultures. The museum's enchanting garden adds to its allure, housing over 600 plants, two ponds with aquatic flora and fauna, rock caves, a stable, a greenhouse, and fountains. Notably, the garden features a Hellenistic temple with a stunning majolica dome and an Egyptian temple. The Stibbert Museum welcomes visitors from Monday to Wednesday, 10 am to 2 pm, and Friday to Sunday, 10 am to 6 pm, with Thursday being the designated closure day. Adult tickets are priced at 8 euros, with discounts available for children. Admission to the whimsical garden is free. It is important to note that a reservation and guide are mandatory for touring the Japanese section, so it is advisable to call ahead to secure a spot. For visitors seeking a blend of history, art, and nature, combining a visit to the Stibbert Museum with nearby attractions such as the historic Villa Fabbricotti and the serene Giardini Baden Powell is highly recommended.

12 – Porcelain Museum

Located within the magnificent Palazzo Pitti in Florence, the Porcelain Museum offers a captivating exploration of the art of porcelain. Situated in the elevated Boboli Gardens, this museum showcases a collection of over 2,000 meticulously crafted porcelain pieces. While the quantity may be modest compared to other renowned museums in Florence, the museum's focus on quality and intricate details is truly captivating. Beyond its role as a gallery, the Porcelain Museum serves as a historical testament, tracing the evolution of Florentine rulers over a span of 250 years, from the Medici era to the Unification of Italy in the mid-1800s.

The museum's collection features exquisite works from renowned porcelain manufacturers such as Doccia Manufactory, Sèvres, and Meissen. The carefully curated rooms, set amidst the stunning gardens, showcase a diverse array of porcelain items, ranging from vases and dinner sets to sculptures and small trinkets. The collection includes pieces from the 18th and 19th centuries, not only from Italy but also from countries like Austria, Germany, and France.

A visit to the Porcelain Museum is an affordable treat, as access to this hidden gem is included in the admission ticket for the Boboli Gardens. Furthermore, the museum offers splendid panoramic views of the surrounding countryside, enhancing the overall experience. If you plan to explore multiple Florentine museums, consider opting for a combination ticket to maximize your cultural immersion.

The Porcelain Museum is open daily from 8:15 am to 6:30 pm, allowing ample time to explore its intriguing collection. Don't forget to allocate some additional time to wander through the lush Boboli Gardens and appreciate their natural beauty.

13 – Museum of the Medici Chapels

Situated within the grand San Lorenzo complex in Florence, the Museum of the Medici Chapels offers an enriching experience filled with beauty, history, and remarkable art. The complex, which encompasses the monumental San Lorenzo church, holds great significance as one of the largest church complexes in Florence and the oldest in the city, with a history dating back to 393 AD.

Georgia Tucker

The basilica itself holds immense importance to the people of Florence, serving as the final resting place for numerous members of the influential Medici family, who exerted significant patronage over the arts and held considerable power in the city for centuries. Cosimo de Medici, in particular, played a pivotal role in shaping the San Lorenzo complex, commissioning renowned architect Brunelleschi to design the magnificent Laurentian Library adjacent to the church.

Within the complex, the Museum of the Medici Chapels stands as a testament to Florentine history and artistry. The chapels, namely the Sagrestia Nuova ("New Sacristy") and the Cappella dei Principi ("Chapel of the Princes"), exude immaculate design and house tombs of individuals who played significant roles in Florence's history. The Sagrestia Nuova, designed by Michelangelo in the 1520s, showcases sculptures such as Day, Night, Dawn, and Dusk, flanking the tombs of Lorenzo and Giuliano Medici. The larger Cappella dei Principi, a project spanning centuries and completed in the 20th century, impresses visitors with its grand dome and the tombs of six Medici Grand Dukes.

Upon entering the chapels from the rear of the church, visitors are greeted by stunning frescoes adorning the walls and ceilings, painted by revered Florentine artists. The museum also houses a diverse collection of paintings and artifacts that complement the rich cultural heritage on display.

The museum ticket, priced at 18.5 euros, grants access not only to the awe-inspiring Medici Chapels but also includes entry to the Laurentian Library and the rest of the San Lorenzo complex. While exploring the area, take the opportunity to visit the Medici-Riccardi Palace, a magnificent example of Renaissance architecture. Additionally, indulge in an authentic Italian meal paired with a glass of wine at one of the nearby trattorias, such as Trattoria Zà Zà or Trattoria Dall'Oste.

14 – Gucci Garden

Attention fashion enthusiasts! Prepare to be enthralled by the Gucci Garden, an exclusive museum nestled in the vibrant tourist district of Florence. Unlike its Hollywood counterpart, the "House of Gucci" with its star-studded cast, this lesser-known museum stands as the genuine embodiment of Gucci's legacy, located right in the heart of the city's bustling atmosphere.

Housed in the 13th-century Palazzo della Mercanzia, adjacent to the Palazzo Vecchio, the Gucci Garden spans three floors and serves as a captivating tribute to one of the world's most iconic luxury fashion brands. It offers visitors a comprehensive journey through Gucci's evolution, from its humble beginnings as a small leather goods workshop in 1921 to its present-day status as a global haute couture powerhouse. The museum's interactive exhibits engage both fashion enthusiasts and non-enthusiasts alike, providing insights into the creation of Gucci's famous "GG" logo and showcasing iconic designs worn by Oscar winners and celebrities during the early 2000s.

In addition to its ever-changing gallery space featuring a diverse range of handbags, outfits, scarves, luggage, and memorabilia, the museum boasts a charming garden where visitors can enjoy a leisurely picnic or a delightful evening glass of wine. Before departing, don't forget to stop by the gift shop and acquire some Gucci-branded treasures to commemorate your visit.

Notably, the Gucci Garden upholds the brand's high standards by housing one of Florence's finest restaurants. Created by three-Michelin-starred chef Massimo Bottura, the 50-seat Gucci Osteria elevates American classics to a sophisticated level, providing a tantalizing dining experience. If your primary intention is to savor the culinary delights, a complimentary museum ticket will accompany your meal.

15 – Galileo Museum

If you ask any science enthusiast who has explored the Jewel of the Renaissance, they will enthusiastically endorse the Galileo Museum as one of the premier museums in Florence. This captivating museum, situated within the historical Museo di Storia della Scienza (Museum of the History of Science), goes beyond its dedication to the renowned scientist Galileo. It offers an interactive and educational experience suitable for both children and adults, covering various aspects of Galileo's life, his inventions, and his controversial clash with the church over his heliocentric theory.

At the Galileo Museum, visitors can delve into the remarkable discoveries and contributions made by Galileo, marvel at his original instruments and writings, and explore a wide range of scientific tools dating back to the 13th century, including barometers, globes, and microscopes. The museum even showcases fragments of the great astronomer himself, including his famous missing fingers. Interactive exhibits provide opportunities to experiment with light and sound while engaging displays test visitors' knowledge of astronomy.

Conveniently located along the picturesque riverfront of Florence, the Galileo Museum offers a perfect opportunity to spend a half-day immersing oneself in scientific history. Nearby attractions such as the Uffizi Gallery, Ponte Vecchio, and the Giardino Bardini (Bardini Gardens) await exploration, making the area a captivating destination for history enthusiasts and inquisitive minds.

Georgia Tucker

The museum operates from 9:30 am to 6 pm daily, except on Tuesdays when it closes at 1 pm. Admission tickets are reasonably priced at 11 euros for adults, and children under six can enter for free.

16 – Palazzo Medici Riccardi

Ever contemplated the experience of entering an authentic 15th-century palace and beholding the intricate details of a ruling family's private abode? The Palazzo Medici Riccardi, renowned as one of Florence's finest museums, offers a rare opportunity to glimpse into the opulent lifestyle of an aristocratic lineage through its resplendent chandeliers and priceless artworks. Originally constructed in 1444 for the prominent Medici family, this grandiose palace now houses a remarkable collection of artwork, including masterpieces by esteemed artists such as Donatello, Filippo Lippi, and Benozzo Gozzoli. Moreover, the museum showcases an extensive array of ancient sculptures, displayed throughout the home museum and its enchanting Walled Garden. Notably, the Gallery features a breathtaking painted ceiling executed by the brush of Luca Giordano, depicting eight episodes of mythological scenes on its walls, reminiscent of the renowned beauty of the Vatican's Sistine Chapel. To make the most of your visit to this extraordinary example of early Renaissance architecture, a guided tour, led by knowledgeable locals well-versed in art and history, is highly recommended. These tours operate on Saturdays and Sundays at 3 pm, guiding visitors through lavishly adorned rooms filled with artworks, furniture, tapestries, and more, while regaling tales of the fascinating history of the Medici family — from their humble origins as medieval bankers to their eventual ascent as one of

Europe's most influential dynasties. A visit to the Palazzo Medici Riccardi is essential for anyone intrigued by Florence's rich history, and exploring the various rooms and artworks can easily occupy a few hours. Moreover, its proximity to the Basilica of San Lorenzo and the Medici Chapels allows for convenient back-to-back activities, making it an ideal addition to your itinerary. The palace welcomes visitors from Monday to Saturday, between 9 am and 7 pm, except for Wednesdays. Standard entry tickets are priced at 7 euros for access to the museums, 10 euros for access to the museum and rotating exhibition, and an additional 4 euros for the guided tour.

17 – San Marco Museum

For those captivated by the life and works of Fra Angelico, one of Florence's most celebrated figures — a painter, architect, sculptor, and true Renaissance polymath — a visit to the San Marco Museum is an absolute must. Housed within the former convent of San Marco, which once served as the residence and workplace of Angelico himself under the patronage of the esteemed Cosimo de' Medici, this splendidly transformed monastery now hosts a magnificent museum. It showcases not only Angelico's renowned creations but also artworks by other artists who resided and worked in the convent over the centuries, representing a diverse selection of artistic talent. While one could spend hours perusing the museum's halls and courtyard, a standout masterpiece is undoubtedly Fra Angelico's "Annunciation," considered one of his most exceptional works and one of the last frescoes completed at San Marco. Depicting the moment when the angel Gabriel appears to Mary, this painting stands as a masterpiece of 15th-century Italian art.

Other beloved attractions include the First Floor Dormitories and the mesmerizing Chapter House, originally a space where monks gathered for congregations, now adorned with depictions of the Crucifixion and Saints adorning its walls. However, the allure of the San Marco Museum extends beyond its art collection, as the venue itself is a work of art. Dating back to the 15th century (though occupied since the 12th century), the monastery showcases exquisite medieval architecture, with frescoes in the cloister meticulously executed by 16th-century Italian Mannerist painter Poccetti, depicting scenes from the daily life of San Marco and providing glimpses into the bygone era. Nestled in the northern part of Florence, a leisurely 10 to 15-minute walk from the main historic sites, the San Marco Museum opens its doors from Monday to Friday, 8.15 am to 1.15 pm, and on weekends from 8.15 am to 4.15 pm. Advanced booking is highly recommended for guided tours, which offer invaluable insights into the museum's treasures.

18 – Museo Novecento

Craving a change of pace from the dominance of Renaissance art and continuous immersion in Florence's historical narrative? Look no further than the Museo Novecento, an art museum dedicated to the Italian art of the 20th century. As the name suggests, this museum houses a remarkable collection of significant artistic works from the modern era, many of which were graciously donated to the city following the devastating Florence flood of 1966. Challenging the notion that Florence is solely the cradle of the Renaissance, the museum's collection encompasses three hundred works displayed across fifteen exhibition rooms. Notable artists featured include representatives of the Futurist movement, such as Giorgio Morandi, Mario Mafai, Renato Guttuso, Giorgio De Chirico, Filippo De Pisis, Gino Severini, and Felice Casorati, among others. The museum also showcases the highly regarded Alberto Della Ragione collection, along with a range of interactive activities that promote engagement with the artworks, including meditation sessions, guided tours for both adults and children, one-person exhibitions, and documentary showcases. Conveniently situated opposite the Piazza Santa Maria Novella, a significant square in Florence and a popular meeting point for city walking tours (strongly recommended!), the Museo Novecento boasts a minimalist design that provides a refreshing contrast to the layers of history found in other Florence museums. This aesthetic allows visitors to immerse themselves fully in the contemplation and appreciation of each artwork. Admission to the museum is priced at 9.50 euros for adults, with discounted rates available for students and seniors. The museum is open every day except Thursday, from 11 am to 8 pm.

19 – Museo di Palazzo Davanzati

Dating back to the mid-14th century, the Palazzo Davanzati stands as one of Florence's oldest structures. Painstakingly preserved to depict life in the Middle Ages, it offers a captivating and invaluable glimpse into the domestic arrangements and affluent lifestyle of a typical wealthy family of that era. Throughout its eventful history, the palace changed hands between the Davizzi family, the original builders, and the subsequent Davanzati family, who retained ownership until the mid-1800s. In 1904, the Antique Dealer Elia Volpi acquired and meticulously restored the premises, establishing the Museum of the Old Florentine House, which has since welcomed visitors.

Consequently, the Palazzo now epitomizes aristocratic narratives, providing guests with insights into the medieval existence in Florence during the city's artistic zenith. Furnished with original pieces from the 14th and 15th centuries, as well as replicas of furnishings and tools such as woodworking instruments, looms, warping machines, and spinning wheels, the tower's three floors can only be accessed through guided tours. Yet, considering the wealth of history encapsulated within these walls, this mode of exploration is undoubtedly the most fitting. Among the vibrant rooms, characterized by colored tiles and intricate frescoes, the Sala dei Pappagalli (The Parrots Room), with its expansive fireplace and abundant bird-themed artwork, as well as the Bedroom adorned with scenes from the life of the Lady of Vergi, stand out as aesthetically captivating spaces. Together, these rooms offer glimpses into the fashion, trends, and everyday lives of the haute couture of centuries past. The Museo di Palazzo Davanzati welcomes visitors from Monday to Sunday, between 8.15 am and 1.50 pm, with an admission fee of merely 2 euros, making it an incredibly affordable destination.

20 – The Leonardo da Vinci Museum
Undoubtedly, the Leonardo da Vinci Museum stands as one of the finest institutions in Florence for individuals with a penchant for innovation, aspiring scientists, and devoted historians seeking to immerse themselves in an era of unparalleled ingenuity and advancement.

As its name suggests, this museum is exclusively dedicated to the incomparable Leonardo da Vinci, the renowned painter, sculptor, architect, musician, and scientist who prolifically produced a multitude of inventions during his lifetime spanning from 1452 to 1519.

Within the museum, a remarkable collection of da Vinci's notebooks and manuscripts are meticulously preserved and put on display, allowing visitors to witness his genius firsthand. Additionally, a copy of the famed Vitruvian Man and various models of his groundbreaking inventions, most of which were far ahead of their time, captivate the imagination of onlookers.

The exhibition is thoughtfully organized into five sections, four of which are inspired by da Vinci's study of the natural elements— earth, wind, fire, and water—while the fifth section focuses on his ingenious and innovative mechanisms.

During the summer season, the Leonardo da Vinci Museum welcomes visitors daily from 9:30 am to 7:30 pm for 8 euros for adults. In the winter months, the museum operates from November to March, opening from Monday to Friday between 10:30 am and 6:30 pm, and on weekends from 9:30 am to 7:30 pm. Tickets can be purchased at a rate of 8 euros per person or 28 euros for a family ticket, which includes admission for two adults and two children.

For those seeking a more in-depth exploration of the legendary inventor's life, works, and achievements, guided tours are available in Italian, English, and French. It is advisable to book these tours in advance to ensure availability.

21 – The Leonardo Interactive Museum

Dedicated to providing visitors with an interactive and immersive experience, the modern Leonardo Interactive Museum allows inquisitive and playful guests to test and operate actual working machines and mechanisms designed by the genius himself. This Leonardo-themed museum, with a focus on families, is conveniently located near the larger Leonardo da Vinci Museum on Via de Servi, on the northern side of Florence.

Featuring a rich assortment of interactive machines meticulously designed and constructed by Leonardo or based on his original designs and drawings, this institution is a treasure trove for young and curious minds. Divided into four distinct themed zones—earth, water, air, and fire, in classic da Vinci style—the museum showcases an array of marvels, including flying machines, robots, hydraulic pumps, and siege engines. It offers an abundance of hands-on experiences, leaving budding inventors spoiled for choice.

However, the museum also caters to adults with captivating exhibits on Leonardo's life and accomplishments as an artist, scientist, and thinker. Original manuscripts, alongside high-quality replicas and digital renditions of his most famous paintings such as The Last Supper, adorn the museum, making it a must-visit for art enthusiasts. Noteworthy are Leonardo's cartographic skills, represented by a dedicated section showcasing 20 exquisite geographical drawings within the 400-square-meter building.

In summary, the Leonardo Interactive Museum is a small yet significant museum that caters to families, offering an enjoyable and educational experience for both children and adults. With an affordable admission fee of 7 euros per adult and discounted rates for children, it presents an engaging opportunity to delve

Georgia Tucker

into the exceptional works of the renowned inventor, painter, and iconic historical figure. Families seeking a brief but delightful and enriching indoor activity will undoubtedly find delight in this museum.

TIPS FOR VISITING THE MUSEUMS IN FLORENCE

Before delving into the list of the top museums in Florence, it is essential to provide some useful tips for those planning to visit these cultural institutions.

Skip The Line Tickets

It is crucial to note that the most popular museums in Florence often have long queues, particularly during peak tourism months, although lines can form at any time of the year. Surely, a visit to Florence should not be marred by spending hours standing in lines. Therefore, it is highly recommended to invest a little extra and opt for skip-the-line tickets.

The Uffizi Gallery and the Accademia Gallery, in particular, attract significant crowds and warrant the purchase of timed entry tickets. You can conveniently book an Uffizi Gallery timed ticket here and an Accademia Gallery timed ticket here.

Other Florence museums may also experience queues, although not as lengthy as those at the aforementioned galleries. To ensure a seamless experience during busy periods, it is advisable to book skip-the-line tickets for the Medici Chapels, the Boboli Gardens, the Pitti Palace, and the Palazzo Vecchio. These tickets can be acquired here.

Guided tours are often offered at these museums, providing a valuable opportunity to gain insights and enjoy priority access. Further details about guided tours will be discussed concerning each specific site.

Closed Days

Another important consideration is that many prominent museums in Florence close for one day each week. For instance, the Uffizi Gallery and the Accademia Gallery are closed on Mondays. The Medici Chapels are closed on Tuesdays, as well as certain Sundays. The Palazzo Vecchio closes on Thursday afternoons. It is advisable to review the closure schedules of each museum when planning your visit. However, rest assured that Florence boasts numerous alternative museums to explore, allowing for flexible trip planning.

City Cards For Florence

Furthermore, it is worth mentioning that Florence offers several cards or combination tickets that can provide cost savings for those intending to visit multiple museums. The Firenze Card, priced at €85, offers fast-track entry to over 50 museums, including the major ones, within 72 hours. If you plan on extensive sightseeing, this card can offer considerable value.

While other companies are offering Florence city passes, it is not recommended to pursue them due to their limited value and benefits. Alternatively, individual museums often provide attractive combo tickets. The Bargello Museums, for instance, offer a pass allowing access to all five of their sites for just €18, a significant reduction compared to purchasing individual tickets. Other examples include combined tickets for the Uffizi Gallery, Pitti Palace, and Boboli Gardens, available at €38 instead of €46.

These tips and insights will assist you in planning a rewarding and seamless museum visitation experience in Florence.

THE 15 BEST BEACHES NEAR FLORENCE, ITALY (2023)

Renowned for its architectural marvels and cultural richness, Florence, the capital of Tuscany, offers a unique opportunity to explore not only its captivating cityscape but also some of Italy's finest coastal destinations. Immerse yourself in the allure of Italian sandy beaches while basking in the warm sun. Discover the best beaches near Florence and embark on an unforgettable seaside experience.

WHAT ARE THE BEST BEACHES NEAR FLORENCE?

A multitude of picturesque beaches lies within easy reach. For those seeking proximity to Florence, Viareggio, Marina di Pisa, and Castiglioncello stand as prime choices. If you are willing to venture further, Bocca d'Arno presents an excellent option.

ARE THERE ANY BEACHES IN FLORENCE?
Florence itself is not situated on the coastline. Nevertheless, numerous exquisite beaches near the city provide ample opportunities to savor Italy's stunning coastal landscapes.

WHAT BEACH IS CLOSEST TO FLORENCE ITALY?
The closest beach to Florence is Viareggio, located approximately 62 miles away from the city.

HOW TO GET TO THE BEACH FROM FLORENCE?
Various transportation options facilitate access to the beaches from Florence, including bus services, train rides, and private vehicles. The most suitable mode of transportation depends on your location and preferred travel distance.

Here are our recommendations for the top beaches near Florence:

1. The Beaches At Viareggio (Best For Distance From Florence)
Situated in Tuscany, Viareggio is a captivating coastal city located just an hour away from Florence. Offering breathtaking views of the western coast, this 10km stretch of shoreline boasts pristine sandy beaches, providing ample space for relaxation and swimming. The beachfront also features an array of charming eateries and cafes, allowing visitors to savor delightful meals and

beverages while admiring the azure sea. Notably, the promenade encompasses several points of interest, including a lighthouse offering panoramic vistas of the Mediterranean Ocean.

Getting there from Florence:

Fastest – Drive (1h 3m)

Alternative – Train (1h 42m) The public beach is close to the train station

2. The Beach At Marina Di Pisa (Best For Families And Kids)

Marina di Pisa, a former fishing village transformed into a coastal resort, beckons travelers seeking a family-friendly beach experience. Located approximately 12km from Pisa, famous for its leaning tower, Marina di Pisa features a wide sandy shore and shallow waters. Although the waters may be less transparent compared to other beaches, this destination offers a delightful escape from the city, allowing visitors to indulge in the seaside ambiance.

Getting there from Florence:

Fastest – Drive by car (1h 12m)

Alternative – Train (1h 21m)

3. The Beach At Castiglioncello (Best For Caves And Cliff Views)

Positioned about an hour and a half away from Florence in the province of Livorno, Castiglioncello allures beachgoers with its charming seaside village ambiance. Highly favored by Italians, this coastal town captivates visitors with its unspoiled beauty, secluded among cliffs and coves. The beach offers a combination of sandy stretches and rocky areas, with pristine waters perfect for swimming and snorkeling. Moreover, Castiglioncello provides a variety of attractions, including a promenade, a pine tree forest, and vibrant summer festivals.

Getting there from Florence:

- Fastest – Drive by car (1h 24m)
- Alternative – Train (1h 32m)

4. Bocca D'arno (Best For A Day Trip)

Situated near Marina di Pisa, Bocca d'Arno stretches along the coastline, offering an idyllic setting for swimming, sunbathing, and surfing. As one of Livorno's most popular destinations, this beach features numerous beach clubs, restaurants, and cafes catering to visitors. The crystal-clear waters further enhance the allure, making it an ideal spot for snorkeling.

Getting there from Florence:

- Fastest – Drive by car (1h 32m)
- Alternative – Train and bus (1h 37m)

5. Antignano Beach (Best For Rocky Landscape)

Antignano, a charming village located approximately an hour away from Florence in Livorno, reveals a wide pebbly beach. While swimming may not be the primary attraction due to the rocky terrain, the mesmerizing rocky landscape offers a unique allure. If you plan to swim, it is advisable to bring rubber shoes for the water. Additionally, the village is home to a variety of restaurants and cafes, allowing visitors to savor local cuisine.

Getting there from Florence:

- Fastest – Drive (1h 15m)
- Alternative – Train (1h 45m)

6. San Vincenzo (Best For Kitesurfing)

These beaches near Florence promise unforgettable moments of relaxation, natural beauty, and coastal exploration. Choose the one that aligns with your preferences and embark on an enchanting seaside getaway.

San Vincenzo, renowned for its excellent kitesurfing opportunities, is a charming village situated along the picturesque Etruscan Coast in the Province of Livorno. Boasting expansive sandy beaches and crystalline waters, this locale offers an idyllic setting for beach enthusiasts. The village exudes a vibrant ambiance, with numerous cafes dotting the area. For strolls or invigorating runs, the promenade presents an inviting pathway.

San Vincenzo is a favored destination for windsurfing, kitesurfing, and delightful boat rides. Aspiring enthusiasts can avail themselves of several schools in the vicinity, providing both lessons and equipment rentals. Among the popular beaches in San Vincenzo, Rimigliano Beach stands out, attracting visitors for its natural beauty. Moreover, hiking enthusiasts find delight in the region's scenic trails.

Traveling from Florence to San Vincenzo:

Fastest option – By car, the journey takes approximately 1 hour and 34 minutes.

Alternative option – By train, the travel time is approximately 1 hour and 54 minutes.

7. Marina Di Bibbona (Best For Turtle Spotting)

Marina di Bibbona, nestled in the province of Livorno, is a tranquil village that offers an enchanting coastal experience. The beach at Bibbona boasts fine sand, complemented by the presence of majestic pine trees, embodying the essence of Italy's natural coastal beauty. The beach's crystal-clear waters have been awarded the prestigious blue flag for their cleanliness, inviting visitors to partake in activities such as kayaking and paddling. Additionally, the area serves as a habitat for loggerhead turtles, attracting wildlife enthusiasts who wish to witness these fascinating creatures laying their eggs.

Traveling from Florence to Marina di Bibbona:

Fastest option – By car, the journey takes approximately 1 hour and 27 minutes.

Alternative option – By train and bus, the travel time is approximately 2 hours and 34 minutes.

8. Marina Di Cecina (Best For Surfing)

Marina di Cecina, a peaceful village nestled between the rolling hills of Tuscany and the azure Mediterranean Sea, offers a serene coastal retreat. While exuding a sense of tranquility, the village's beautiful beaches thrive with activity during the summer months. Surfing enthusiasts particularly appreciate the favorable waves during the winter season. Furthermore, Marina di Cecina provides ample open spaces and family-oriented activities, ensuring a memorable experience for visitors. Notably, the village is also home to Aquapark, one of Italy's largest waterparks.

Traveling from Florence to Marina di Cecina:

Fastest option – By car, the journey takes approximately 1 hour and 23 minutes.

Alternative option – By train, the travel time is approximately 1 hour and 41 minutes.

9. The Beach In Baratti Gulf (Best For Ancient Ruins)

The Beach in Baratti Gulf, renowned for its ancient Etruscan ruins, is situated within the small bay between the Ligurian Sea and the Tyrrhenian Sea, north of the peninsula, and lies adjacent to the promontory of Populonia and Torraccia, part of the municipality of San Vincenzo. The coastline offers a blend of pristine and developed beaches, catering to various preferences. Umbrella and chair rentals are available for those seeking comfort and convenience. Notably, Baratti Gulf was once a bustling Etruscan port, with a primary focus on iron processing. Today, visitors to Baratti Beach may catch glimpses of black and silver fragments glimmering in the sand, remnants of the iron processing activities that transpired long ago.

Traveling from Florence to the Beach in Baratti Gulf:

Fastest option – By car, the journey takes approximately 2 hours and 12 minutes.

Alternative option – By train, bus, and a 2-kilometer walk, the travel time is approximately 3 hours.

10. Cala Violina Beach (Best For A Quiet Day)

Cala Violina Beach, situated within the scenic natural reserve of Le Bandite di Scarlino in Maremma, lies between Follonica and Punta Ala. This beach is renowned for its clear waters, soft white sand, and unspoiled natural beauty. Nestled amidst promontories, Cala Violina offers a tranquil setting for those seeking a serene and relaxing beach experience. The beach derives its name from the unique sound emitted when walking on its sand, which resembles the melodious notes of a violin. To fully appreciate this enchanting phenomenon, it is recommended to visit during quieter periods, as the beach can become crowded in the summer months. Please note that accessing the beach requires a 2-kilometer walk or bike ride, which may be slightly challenging. While the beach is narrow and elongated, it remains largely undeveloped, so visitors are advised to bring a picnic basket. During the summer season, a food truck may be available for refreshments.

Traveling from Florence to Cala Violina Beach:

Fastest option – By car and walking to access the beach, the journey takes approximately 2 hours and 5 minutes.

Alternative option – By train, taxi, and walking, the travel time is approximately 2 hours and 38 minutes.

11. Giglio Island Beach (Best For Snorkeling)

Isola del Giglio, situated in the province of Grosseto, boasts a captivating coastline spanning 28km, adorned with secluded coves, cliffs, and numerous beaches. Among them, Spiaggia Campese stands as Giglio's largest beach, featuring a picturesque cliff and an ancient tower. Notably, the reddish-colored sand adds a unique charm to the beach, complemented by breathtaking sunset views. Coffee shops along the shoreline offer delightful moments of relaxation. For snorkeling enthusiasts, Spiaggia della Canella provides an excellent spot surrounded by rocks, creating a natural aquarium. The combination of limestone cliffs and white sand makes it one of Giglio's most stunning beaches, although it tends to be more crowded.

Getting there from Florence:

Fastest – Drive and Ferry (3h 30m)

12. Forte Dei Marmi Beach (Best Beach For Kids)

Located in the coastal town of Forte dei Marmi, within the province of Tuscany, Forte dei Marmi Beach serves as a favored destination for families, offering a wide array of activities and amenities. The beach club provides well-equipped facilities, including showers, toilets, a playground, and a dedicated kids' play area. Moreover, the beach attracts surfers, with locals often visiting to enjoy the waves.

Getting there from Florence:

- Fastest – Drive by car (1h 31)
- Alternative – Train and bus (2h)

13. Lido Di Camaiore (Best For Windsurfing)

Nestled in the town of Camaiore, situated in the province of Tuscany, Lido di Camaiore stands out as a popular beach for windsurfing. Enthusiasts flock to this destination to harness the coastal winds. The beach also offers opportunities for swimming and sunbathing, accompanied by a selection of restaurants and cafes along the shoreline.

Getting there from Florence:

- Fastest – Drive (1h 15m)

- Alternative – Train and bus (2h 21m)

14. Marina Di Massa (Best For Scuba Diving)

Marina di Massa, located in the town of Massa within the province of Tuscany, allures scuba diving enthusiasts with its vibrant underwater world. The beach also offers opportunities for swimming and sunbathing, accompanied by a variety of restaurants and cafes to enhance your seaside experience.

Getting there from Florence:

- Fastest – Drive(1h 15m)

- Alternative – Train and bus (2h 31m)

15. Isola D' Elba (Best For Snorkeling)

Elba Island, the third-largest island in Italy, forms part of the Tuscan Archipelago and lies in the Tyrrhenian Sea. With its sprawling landscape, it takes over an hour to traverse the island from end to end, offering an abundance of captivating beaches to explore. Elba Island presents a natural oasis of beauty, characterized by crystal-clear waters, private beaches, hiking trails, and breathtaking vistas. Although accessing the island requires a bit more effort, involving a ferry journey, the stunning scenery and pristine waters of Elba Island make it well worth the trip.

Getting there from Florence:

- Fastest – Drive and Ferry (3h)
- Alternative – Bus and Fly (3h)

Embark on an unforgettable journey to these enchanting beach destinations near Florence, where each offers its unique blend of natural wonders, recreational activities, and coastal charm.

Georgia Tucker

CHAPTER SEVEN

WHERE TO GO SHOPPING IN FLORENCE

Shopping in Florence offers a captivating experience, as the city boasts an array of streets, neighborhoods, and shops that are truly worth exploring. Florence holds a significant position in the realm of fashion, making shopping a pivotal aspect of the city's identity. Renowned for its high-end status, Florence presents a magnificent parade of design houses, iconic brands, and establishments that have mastered the art of perfection in their aesthetic appeal. Whether you seek to enhance your style or discover exquisite garments, Florence stands as an ideal destination to fulfill your desires.

Contrary to popular belief, Florence offers more than just luxury shopping. The city is renowned for its rich textile heritage and artisanal crafts, fostering a culture of creativity and innovation. Consequently, Florence is home to a diverse selection of boutiques and stores that cater to various tastes. The city exudes an unparalleled sense of style, further enhanced by its medieval attractions and flourishing restaurant scene. Thus, indulging in a shopping spree in Florence becomes an absolute delight, combining elegance and cultural allure.

BEST SHOPPING IN FLORENCE

1. Via Roma And Via Dei Calzaiuoli

These two streets serve as Florence's primary shopping hub, bridging the iconic Duomo and the central square of Piazza della Signoria. Via Roma hosts prestigious brands like Miu Miu, Armani, and the renowned luxury destination, Luisa via Roma. Established in 1930, Luisa via Roma showcases the latest designs from luxury labels such as Valentino and Fendi. Adjacent to Via Roma, La Rinascente department store presents six floors dedicated to fashion and homewares, complete with a roof terrace offering a refreshing post-shopping experience. Via dei Calzaiuoli houses an array of high-street labels, including Calzedonia and the retail outlet Coin.

2. Via Dei Serragli

Located across the Arno River, the Oltrarno district is celebrated for its artisan workshops. Here, avid shoppers can explore clothing at Frame, leather goods at Quoio, and a mix of clothing and vintage home accessories at Indigo Mood (temporarily closed). To cover all shopping bases, indulge in locally made hats and shoes at Reinhard Plank and exquisite jewelry at Nokike Atelier.

3. Via De' Tornabuoni

A must-visit for fashion enthusiasts seeking designer labels, Via de' Tornabuoni showcases the crème de la crème of fashion, including Gucci, Pucci, and Prada. The pedestrianized street exudes elegance, encouraging leisurely window shopping. Don't miss the opportunity to explore the sensory experience at Olfattorio Bar a Parfums, a cosmetic store, and delve into the basement of Palazzo Spini Feroni, home to Ferragamo, where you can embark on a journey through the history of shoemaking since the 1920s.

4. Borgo Santi Apostoli

A charming cobbled lane adjacent to Via de' Tornabuoni, Borgo Santi Apostoli is where legendary local designer Angela Caputi showcases her bold contemporary jewelry, meticulously kept in velvet-lined drawers. Across the street, the shoe brand Viajiyu offers made-to-order shoes, allowing customers to choose their style, color, and trim, with worldwide shipping available.

5. Via Della Vigna Nuova

Stretching south from Via de' Tornabuoni towards the Arno River, Via della Vigna Nuova presents an enticing collection of clothing stores that culminate at the leather outlet Benheart. This outlet offers jackets, bags, and accessories crafted with genuine dedication by a Florence-based designer. For unique homewares, Mario Luca Giusti's acrylic glasses and bowls make for delightful souvenirs that bring a touch of vibrancy to any room.

6. Via Della Spada

In recent years, Via della Spada has emerged as a notable shopping destination. This street offers an ideal blend of fashion and home decor, featuring sustainable and quirky offerings at the MIO Concept Store.

7. Via Romana

Linking Palazzo Pitti to Porta Romana, Via Romana is home to Muselab and Be Giuls, where hand-stitched clothing can be discovered, as well as Reciclo, offering upcycled furniture and unique T-shirts by John Rocket. Sdrucciolo de' Pitti, a charming side street connecting Piazza de' Pitti to Piazza Santo Spirito, is worth a detour for its bold prints at Giulia Materia and the Sicilian couture at Tiziana Alemanni.

8. Via Maggio

Traditionally renowned for its antique stores, Via Maggio now showcases a fusion of street fashion and art shops nestled within the ground floors of Renaissance palaces. Dexter is a go-to destination for curated men's and women's wear.

Georgia Tucker

9. Via De' Bardi And Via Di San Niccolò
Heading east, visitors will discover handcrafted paper creations by Erin Ciulla at Il Torchio, a unique studio-store housing leather notebooks and marbled paper. On Via di San Niccolò, Alessandro Dari's fine jewelry atelier presents a captivating blend of museum-like pieces and exquisite silver jewelry. Additionally, perfume enthusiasts can visit Sileno Cheloni's eponymous space, where private sessions allow shoppers to create their bespoke fragfragranceszr those seeking bespoke shoes, Stefano Bemer offers artisan-crafted footwear within the confines of an old church workshop, beneath the shadow of Torre San Niccolò.

10. Via Di Santo Spirito And Via Dello Sprone
For the latest contemporary designs, Santo Spirito 9 by local designer Federico Curradi is a must-visit. Delight in his cashmere sweaters and unique artisanal pieces. Angela Caputi's flagship store features drawers filled with enticing jewelry waiting to be explored, while Francesco offers timeless gladiator-style leather sandals. On Via dello Sprone, Bjørk showcases chic and streamlined Nordic designs, while Sara Amrhein Firenze presents colorful jewelry crafted with polymer clay and beading, ideal for the spring season.

11. The Mall Firenze
Make sure not to overlook The Mall Firenze, a renowned destination for discounted designer labels, as you curate your itinerary. Nestled amidst the verdant hills of Tuscany, this retail village showcases an array of prestigious brands ranging from

Versace and Valentino to Dolce & Gabbana and Roberto Cavalli. Discover last-season styles at a fraction of their original prices, making it a worthwhile excursion beyond the city limits. Conveniently, buses depart every 30 minutes from Santa Maria Novella station, and The Mall Firenze welcomes visitors daily.

I LOVE SHOPPING IN FLORENCE!

Florence Is Shopping!

Once you have immersed yourself in the museums, marveled at the artwork and architecture, and indulged in pizza and gelato, the logical next step is to embark on a shopping spree in Florence. Drawing upon a rich tradition brimming with skilled craftsmen and artisans, Florence emerges as the natural choice for shopping, not only for high fashion but also for unique and one-of-a-kind gifts and souvenirs. Italy's global reputation for exceptional quality and striking design finds a splendid showcase in Florence, and the best part is that you need not strain your budget to indulge in retail therapy. From luxury boutiques featuring top-name designers to fashion outlets, craftsmen workshops, and open-air markets, you are assured of finding precisely what you desire at prices that suit your means.

Window Shopping

While many establishments now adopt "orario continuato," meaning they remain open throughout the day without closing for lunch, some places located farther from the city center still adhere to the practice of opening between 9 and 10 in the morning, closing around 1ish for lunch, only to reopen in the afternoon between 3:30 and 4:30 pm. The good news is that they typically stay open until 7:30-8 pm. Stores generally operate from Monday to Saturday, with Monday mornings and Sundays being typical closure times. If you have specific stores in mind and wish to adhere to a schedule, it is advisable to check the operating hours beforehand.

Another noteworthy aspect is that almost all merchants accept various forms of payment, including cash (Euros), debit cards, and credit cards. It is worth noting, though, that vendors who exclusively accept cash payments typically do not provide receipts. While the choice is yours, bear in mind that being caught with a purchase and no receipt could result in significant fines. Additional fines may be incurred for purchasing items from unauthorized vendors, particularly counterfeit goods. These vendors are often recognizable by their practice of displaying merchandise on easily transportable blankets, bags, or boxes.

Italian Fashion

While Milan is frequently hailed as the fashion capital of Italy, those well-versed in the industry recognize that Florence has undeniably secured its place on the fashion map with Palazzo Pitti's fashion fairs, showcasing cutting-edge and innovative design. The sheer number of top-quality shops and flagship stores stands as a testament to the city's growing significance in the fashion sector.

Since the 14th century, Via Tornabuoni has been home to exquisite and imposing palaces belonging to noble Florentine families such as Antinori and Strozzi. Today, it hosts boutiques for esteemed brands like Gucci, Prada, Pucci, Cartier, and Bulgari, to name a few. This area continues to expand,

Antiques And Collectibles

Florence is renowned for its thriving antique and collectibles scene, with Stefano Bardini being one of the most esteemed dealers in Italy, if not the world. While his museum near Lungo Arno showcases his remarkable collection, local dealers continually strive to match his reputation. When embarking on your browsing journey, Via Maggio and Via de' Fossi are excellent starting points. These streets are brimming with notable antique shops where you can discover valuable artworks and collectibles. The displays in their windows often resemble museum exhibits, showcasing exquisite pieces.

Additionally, there is a collection of antique shops near Piazza Beccaria, usually located in Loggia di Pesce but temporarily relocated to Largo Pietro Annigoni. Here, you can peruse and uncover treasures of various sizes, including items perfectly suited for travel and fitting within your suitcase. Apart from these permanent establishments, Florence offers numerous antique markets that take place on specific dates throughout the city, providing ample opportunities for exploration.

Leather

Florence's proximity to the Arno River has played a significant role in establishing its dominance in the world of leather production and its associated products, such as leather jackets and gloves. The city offers picturesque solutions for leather shopping, including the open-air markets of San Lorenzo and Piazza del Mercato Nuovo, situated between the spacious Piazza Repubblica, Hard Rock Cafe, and the charming Ponte Vecchio.

While the outdoor markets provide a vibrant shopping experience, many stores offer high-quality leather products. It is advisable to compare prices before making a purchase. Wallets, belts, coin purses, and gloves, in particular, are excellent alternatives for acquiring a quality product at a more reasonable price. An exceptional treat awaits those who wish to witness the artisans at work. The Leather School behind Santa Croce and Pierotucci Italian Leather Factory both invite visitors into their workshops, providing an opportunity to observe the creation process firsthand.

Gold, Silver & Art

Even before esteemed artists and sculptors like Brunelleschi, Donatello, Ghiberti, and Botticelli experimented with bronze, silver, and gold, Tuscany boasted skilled Etruscan gold craftsmen. Florence, thanks to Lorenzo de Medici's passion for gold jewelry, became ingrained with this artistry. The tradition of seeking quality pieces on Ponte Vecchio is largely attributed to Ferdinand I.

Aside from its global fame for sparkling jewelry displays, Ponte Vecchio is renowned for its jewelry shops located on the bridge. Here, you can discover a wealth of handmade, unique jewelry items such as necklaces, rings, earrings, bracelets, and pins. Alongside the dazzling offerings, explore the selection of carnelian and sardonyx cameos, as well as the distinctive micro mosaics and artistic compositions known as "Commesso

Fiorentino." These mosaics, created primarily using local marbles, exemplify intricate artwork and serve as true modern masterpieces crafted using an ancient technique.

Perfumes, Ceramics, & Artistic Paper

Florence is home to several historic "pharmacies" specializing in antique recipes or innovative creations with traditional flavors. These establishments produce a wide range of soaps, creams, ambient perfumes, and body fragrances for both men and women. These unique and reasonably priced products make for ideal souvenirs, capturing the essence of Florence.

Another delightful gift option to explore is the exquisite designs on paper. Stationery items feature a combination of colors, swirls, metallic accents, and the iconic Florentine Giglio symbol. The plethora of options includes cards, letters, stationery sets, and large pieces of handcrafted paper, perfect for crafting or gift wrapping.

While most ceramic producers are located outside the city center in areas like Montelupo and Impruneta, Florence boasts a multitude of shops offering a wide selection of artistic bowls, plates, plaques, and souvenirs.

For more comprehensive information on the recommended stores to visit, please refer to our dedicated article.

Food & Wine

Undoubtedly, one of the most sought-after and easily obtainable items to shop for in Florence is its delectable flavors. Some culinary delights, such as bistecca Fiorentina, pizza, and gelato, are best enjoyed on-site and may not travel well. It is advisable to savor these gastronomic delights during your stay. However, there is an abundance of food items that make excellent gifts and memorable souvenirs to share with loved ones upon your return home.

In addition to acquiring products during wine tastings, the covered markets of San Lorenzo and Sant'Ambrogio Market are excellent places to find authentic and genuine products. These markets offer a diverse array of fresh, in-season produce, oils, kinds of pasta, butcher shops, and more. They present an opportunity to procure high-quality items that embody the essence of Florence and Tuscany.

A COMPLETE GUIDE TO SHOPPING FOR LEATHER IN FLORENCE

When it comes to selecting the perfect leather bag or jacket as a cherished souvenir from Florence, the abundance of options can be overwhelming. The sight of numerous jackets fluttering in the breeze at the San Lorenzo market serves as a stark reminder of the daunting nature of leather shopping in Florence. How does one ensure the authenticity and superior quality of a purchase? How does one determine a fair price and avoid being deceived?

Florence offers a multitude of opportunities to acquire leather goods, ranging from luxury boutiques to bustling street bazaars, private workshops, and sidewalk vendors. Read on to discover valuable insights that will enable you to bring home an authentic leather memento to be treasured for a lifetime.

A Centuries-Old Trade

For centuries, Florence and its surrounding region have been renowned for their exceptional leather craftsmanship. However, before the Industrial Revolution, the process of transforming animal hides into leather was considered an unpleasant task. In medieval Florence, tanneries, known as conciatori, were strategically located along the Arno River, facilitating the removal of waste and odors associated with the trade.

By the 1300s, approximately 1,500 shoemakers were already active in the city, with a significant portion settling in the Oltrarno district. These cobblers not only catered to local demand but also engaged in a thriving export trade, laying the foundation for the flourishing Tuscan international leather fashion industry that endures to this day.

In addition to apparel, leather artisans played a vital role in the book trade, producing parchment sheets crafted from cured sheepskins. They also skillfully fashioned leather covers to safeguard books while providing a luxurious and aesthetically pleasing exterior. Furthermore, these artisans pioneered techniques for creating armor, and ceremonial attire, and collaborated with saddle and tack makers to craft regalia for horses used in festivals and daily activities.

In the early twentieth century, the Florentine leather industry reached new heights with the contribution of Guccio Gucci, a native of Florence and the son of a leather craftsman. Departing from the family business, Gucci worked a series of menial jobs at the Savoy Hotel in London, where he handled sophisticated luggage for affluent guests. Returning to Florence in 1921, he redirected his family's focus toward designing exquisite leather luggage and accessories for an international clientele of discerning taste. Gucci swiftly propelled the leather goods of his native city to global fame, establishing his name as one of the most recognizable figures in the fashion world.

How Leather Is Made
The contemporary process of tanning and working leather is considerably more complex than the days of the pungent medieval tanneries along the Arno River. In fact, the production and sale of leather products in Italy encompass a remarkably

intricate domain that intersects with culture, history, fashion, economy, and the essence of Italian identity. To comprehend this multifaceted realm of Italian leather, it is helpful to divide the industry into three distinct tiers:

INDUSTRIAL: The industrial sector employs tens of thousands of individuals and serves as a significant driving force in Italy's economy. Numerous Italian leather jackets, purses, belts, gloves, and shoes available in chic boutiques worldwide originate from enterprises primarily situated outside of Florence. The preparation of hides occurs in small to medium-sized establishments scattered across Tuscany, with a concentration of such enterprises found between Florence and Pisa. Many leather items showcased in Florence's leather shops, or pelletterie, are produced within these medium-sized industrial enterprises in the Tuscan countryside and subsequently distributed to retailers through wholesalers.

LUXURY-BRANDED: These leather goods are crafted for sale in the boutiques of globally recognized Italian luxury brands. This realm is particularly intricate as the perceived value of luxury leather brands heavily relies on the selection and treatment of raw materials, as well as the craftsmanship exhibited in each finished piece. Many luxury companies outsource certain aspects of production to the industrial sector, which also caters to automotive and furniture leather manufacturing. Subcontracting may involve the procurement and preparation of hides, as well as the cutting and stitching of bags, jackets, skirts, dresses, gloves, and other items. However, luxury brands also ensure that specific signature pieces undergo meticulous hand-finishing by skilled artisans in-house. Overall, these luxury-branded items can be viewed as a fusion of industrial and artisanal production since these companies predominantly thrive by selling well-crafted, high-quality products on a large scale.

ARTISANAL: Last but certainly not least, individual artisanal leather producers play a crucial role. Florence is home to numerous skilled and underappreciated leather masters, and it is well worth the effort to seek them out for their exceptional creations and the opportunity to witness their craftsmanship firsthand. Artisanal production primarily focuses on the meticulous art of cutting, fitting, sewing, stitching, and hand-finishing custom works. Today, fully handcrafted leather production in Florence primarily revolves around bookbinding and the creation of small objects such as boxes and desk sets. However, a handful of leather artisans continue to meticulously handcraft gloves, shoes, bags, and other fashion accessories. One notable example is the historic Madova located at Via de' Guicciardini, 1/red.

HOW TO JUDGE LEATHER QUALITY
Envision being able to examine a cross-section of an animal hide under a microscope. The top layer reveals the pores, scars, imperfections, hair follicles, and the hairs themselves. Directly beneath lies a thick, densely woven tissue composed of overlapping fibers. Below that, another layer of fibers appears, less dense and arranged horizontally. Modern processing often involves skimming off these individual layers, and the determination of leather quality is based on subsequent factors:

FULL-GRAIN (PIENO FIORE): Considered the epitome of excellence, full-grain leather represents the top layer of the hide and generally remains unsanded, allowing scars, imperfections, and pores to be visible. This type of leather is coveted for its supple texture, durability, natural aroma, and its ability to develop a beautiful patina over time. Look for the term "pieno fiore" (cuoio pieno fiore or pelle pieno fiore) to identify full-grain leather.

TOP-GRAIN (PARTE GRANO OR CUOIO DI GRANO): Top-grain leather showcases the densely packed grain or pattern of the upper layer of the hide, but it has undergone some sanding to remove certain imperfections. In Italy, there can be some overlap between full-grain and top-grain leather, leading to occasional ambiguity, although top-grain leather is still regarded as high quality.

GENUINE (VERA PELLE OR VERO CUOIO): Genuine leather is sourced from the lower half of the hide and does not display a distinct grain, although it can still possess suppleness, rich color, and a pleasant aroma. Suede is an example of genuine leather.

BONDED (CUOIO RIGENERATO): Bonded leather is a result of the leather-making process byproduct, including dust, shavings, and excess pieces, which are compressed together in the factory using various chemicals, dyes, and glues. It is important to note that bonded leather is often spray-painted to imitate the natural grain of genuine leather. Assessing the scent can help distinguish between genuine leather and bonded leather, as the latter may have a distinct odor of cow or Superglue.

IMITATION: If seeking authentic leather, it is advisable to avoid simipelle (imitation leather). However, for those who abstain from purchasing animal products altogether, ecopelle (a more appealing-sounding term for the same material) may be a preferable alternative.

HOW TO BUY FLORENTINE LEATHER

When it comes to leather bags and apparel, appearances can be deceiving. You may encounter a reasonably priced bag on the street that matches the quality of an item found in a high-end boutique. At times, the same merchant may offer the same bag in both a pelletteria and a market stall, but at significantly different prices. It is not uncommon to find both industrially produced and artisanal pieces sold in the same location.

To ensure acquiring a quality leather souvenir, it is beneficial to be familiar with the tricks of the Florentine leather-shopping trade. Ideally, purchasing directly from the maker provides the best guarantee of knowing the precise nature of the product. However, in Florence, acquiring leather directly from an artisan is primarily feasible for small, portable items such as boxes, wallets, and change purses. Most apparel items are available in small retail shops. In this case, prioritizing the quality of the individual piece rather than the purchase location is crucial. Separate the handbag or jacket from its setting, if possible, and focus on assessing the quality of the item itself.

SELECTING LEATHER GOODS

When evaluating leather quality, it is essential to disregard the bustling street market or the high-end boutique ambiance. Instead, shift your focus away from the buying environment and engage your senses:

AROMA: Trust your sense of smell. Genuine leather should emit a musky and natural scent. Avoid anything that smells like chemicals, as they are often used to treat hides and mask inferior quality.

SUPPLENESS: Genuine leather should feel smooth, supple, and soft, rather than stiff.

COLOR: The finest natural leather in tan or brown does not require added color, as it can exhibit the natural grain and beauty of the material on its own. Dyes, such as red or green, can mask lower-quality leather. If the edges of the leather are unfinished, careful observation can reveal whether the color merely coats the surface or permeates throughout the hide.

STITCHING: Examine the stitching closely. It should be tight, even, and consist of small stitches sewn close together.

For high-quality leather jackets, Benheart is a local favorite. Their knowledgeable staff can provide insights into the craftsmanship and components that contribute to a superior leather piece.

Georgia Tucker

SHOPPING TIPS

As a general guideline, it should be noted that Florentine leather goods are generally priced in a higher range. Nevertheless, they often offer excellent value considering the exceptional quality. Opting to purchase directly from the artisans themselves is the most reliable approach, with a particular focus on smaller, portable items such as boxes, change purses, eyeglass cases, albums, and desk accessories. These items are frequently crafted entirely by hand on-site, and the prices are usually reasonable. Furthermore, they serve as enduring souvenirs and special gifts that are conveniently transportable in your suitcase or can be easily shipped.

It is worth mentioning that Florentine artisans are renowned for their expertise in made-to-measure creations. If you have an interest in acquiring a pair of meticulously handcrafted shoes, Florence offers unparalleled opportunities to not only obtain a stunning pair tailored specifically for you but also to establish a personal connection with the artisan whose labor and passion were invested in fashioning this unique keepsake.

Where To Buy

Florence proudly boasts two bustling outdoor markets that have long been recognized for their diverse selection of leather goods. The San Lorenzo Market features an assortment of street vendors and retail stores offering leather items. The Mercato Nuovo, which has served as an outdoor marketplace since the Renaissance, is also abundant with bags, belts, and other leather products. However, it is advisable to exercise caution when making purchases here.

While market vendors exert considerable efforts to attract travelers, it is important to bear in mind that shopping at these markets can be a challenging endeavor in Florence. The ability to discern higher quality leather from lower quality becomes imperative to ensure a satisfactory purchase that will continue to bring joy upon returning home.

The Mercato Nuovo is also recognized as the "Porcellino" market due to the presence of a popular tourist attraction, a bronze wild boar. While it may be pleasant to stroll through, it is not recommended as a prime location for leather purchases. For a more confident shopping experience, it is advisable to consider the following destinations. Not only will you delve into the history of Florentine leather, but you are also likely to acquire an authentic souvenir that will remain one of the most cherished memories of your journey.

Benheart

Via della Vigna Nuova, 97r; 055/2399483

Via dei Cimatori, 25r; 055/0462638.

Dimitri Villoresi Bags

Via dell'Ardiglione, 22

366/4534867

Digerolamo

Via del Moro, 58

055/2298378

Fratelli Peroni

Via G. Marconi, 82r

055/572520

Gucci Museum

Piazza della Signoria, 10

055/75923302

Leather School

Scuola del Cuoio

Piazza Santa Croce, 16

055/244533

Madova

Via Guicciardini, 1r

055/2396526

Mannina

Via Guicciardini, 16r

055/282895

Monaco Metropolitano

Via dei Ramaglianti, 6r

055/268121

Pelleterie Fiorentine

Georgia Tucker

Via Sant' Egidio, 31/r

055/245335

Roberto Ugolini

Via Michelozzi, 17r

055/216246

Via de' Ginori, 23r (The name of the store is its address!)

055/2398031

Cuor di Pelle

Via dei Pilastri 7A R

+39 3290965746 - +39 055 3880404

A SHOE-BUYING GUIDE IN FLORENCE

Florence is renowned for its rich history and significance in the world of shoes, making it a prime destination for shoe enthusiasts. Since the late 1200s, shoes have held a prominent place in Florentine fashion, showcasing various styles ranging from knee-high boots to elegant Grecian sandals, and crafted from an assortment of materials such as leather and silk, adorned or kept simple. During this period, the export of Florentine shoes thrived, employing numerous cobblers and shoemakers in the city, including a concentration of five hundred on the Oltrarno Street via Street. Additional clusters of cobblers' shops were found in the Santa Croce area along Via dei Pepi, Borgo Allegri, and Via Verdi. Today, some of the finest commercial shoe shops can be found near Piazza della Repubblica on Via degli Speziali.

Handmade and custom-made shoes were the norm until the mid-1800s when factories introduced mass production. Nevertheless, Florence has preserved the art of handmade, bespoke shoes, particularly for men, with several workshops scattered throughout the city. For a glimpse into the world of handmade leather shoes, one can visit Roberto Ugolini's workshop in Piazza Santo Spirito or Saskia in Via Santa Lucia. Additionally, the Salvatore Ferragamo shoe museum offers a fascinating narrative of this modern fashion icon's journey and showcases some of his famous creations.

Salvatore Ferragamo, who initially began his remarkable career as a teenage apprentice, made Florence his home in 1927 after achieving great success in Hollywood, earning him the nickname "shoemaker of the stars." Settling in Florence provided him with easier access to superior materials and skilled artisan cobblers, enabling him to continue creating shoes for renowned American cinema stars, including Audrey Hepburn and Marilyn Monroe. The Ferragamo museum, located in the grand Palazzo Spini-Feroni on via Tornabuoni, has been home to the Ferragamo store and workshop since the 1930s. The museum collection spans from 1927 to 1960, serving as a comprehensive archive of 20th-century fashion.

Georgia Tucker

For those seeking the best leather shoes in Florence, Roberto Ugolini's workshop can be found at Via de' Michelozzi, 17r, Saskia at Via Santa Lucia, 24r, and the Salvatore Ferragamo museum at Via Tornabuoni, 2r.

Georgia Tucker

CHAPTER EIGHT

THE BEST HOTELS IN FLORENCE

Florence boasts an abundance of remarkable artistic and architectural treasures, making it a haven for culture enthusiasts. The city's diverse selection of hotels offers an equally awe-inspiring blend of culture, with many featuring exquisite Renaissance elements and interiors adorned with priceless works of art. These hotels are scattered throughout Florence, catering to various preferences, whether one desires a central location or a tranquil retreat in the surrounding hills. There are also charming guesthouses in the Oltrarno district, a fashionable bohemian area located south of the river, providing a delightful experience without breaking the bank. Without further ado, we present the best hotels in Florence, curated by the editors of Condé Nast Traveller.

HOW WE CHOOSE THE BEST HOTELS IN FLORENCE (TIPS)

Each hotel on this list is independently selected by our editors and reviewed by a Condé Nast Traveller journalist with intimate knowledge of the destination and personal experience staying at the property. In our selection process, we consider a range of properties, including luxury hotels, boutique establishments, and lesser-known hidden gems that offer an authentic and insider's perspective of the destination. We prioritize beautiful design, exceptional location, warm and attentive service, and a commitment to sustainability. This list is regularly updated to include new hotel openings and evolving establishments.

The St Regis Florence

Featured on our 2022 Gold List of the best hotels in the world

Best for: the royal treatment

While Florence boasts a plethora of elegant hotels, something is captivating about The St Regis that entices me to return year after year. Perhaps it's the cozy ambiance that emanates from this 15th-century palazzo adorned with frescoes and crystal chandeliers, offering hidden corners aglow with stained glass, where one can lose oneself for hours with a copy of La Repubblica. The spirit of the Renaissance is never far away, as the original palazzo was designed by Filippo Brunelleschi, the visionary behind the Duomo, and transformed into a hotel in 1866. If the intricately detailed cherubs adorning the ceiling of the Salone delle Feste ballroom could speak, they might recount tales of Botticelli, Amerigo Vespucci (the explorer who named America), as well as Madonna and Keith Richards. However, it's not only the esteemed guests who receive impeccable treatment; the exceptional staff has astoundingly unpacked and ironed my clothes while providing tickets to skip queues at the Diocesan Museum or Santa Maria del Fiore's dome. The rooms, adorned with brocade fabrics and canopied beds, offer picturesque views of the River Arno, while the Winter Garden restaurant provides a reverential dining experience beneath a magnificent glass ceiling.

Georgia Tucker

The St Regis effortlessly blends elegance and warmth, even evidenced by the Christmas tradition of nightly Champagne, where I found myself toasting a giant teddy bear by the fire. At this hotel, the royal treatment is extended to all. - Sara Margo

Address: Piazza Ognissanti, 1, 50123 Firenze FI, Italy

Price: Starting from approximately £410 for double rooms.

Villa San Michele, A Belmond Hotel, Florence
Best for: a bird's eye view of the city

Nestled on a hillside in Fiesole, the Villa San Michele, a Belmond property housed within a 15th-century monastery, exudes a rich historical ambiance. Inspired by the works of Michelangelo, its exquisite Renaissance façade complements the blending of historical elements and contemporary furnishings within its interiors. The former church of the monastery now serves as the reception area, characterized by lofty ceilings and opulent velvet fabrics in deep shades. The transformed cloisters provide a welcoming lounge space adorned with stone columns and lush greenery. The loggia houses two restaurants where every table affords unobstructed vistas of the city below.

At the rear of the property, the meticulously manicured gardens feature multi-level lawns and terraces that offer breathtaking panoramas. An inviting swimming pool of generous proportions provides an idyllic retreat from the bustling tourist crowds. Additionally, historical forest trails on Monte Ceceri, the location of the hotel, allow guests to explore the shaded woodlands where Leonardo da Vinci is said to have conducted the inaugural trial of his "flying machine."

Address: Belmond Villa San Michele, Via Doccia, 4, 50014 Fiesole FI, Italy

Price: Starting from £730 for double rooms

Il Tornabuoni
Best for: shopping

Positioned on the prestigious Via Tornabuoni, Florence's most elegant thoroughfare, Il Tornabuoni is a sophisticated hotel housed in a 13th-century palazzo. Part of the Hyatt portfolio, this property features color-coded floors adorned with vibrant tones such as deep blues, fuchsia, and bright yellows. The walls are adorned with lively depictions of exotic flora and fauna, paying homage to the Renaissance era, featuring butterflies, monkeys, beetles, and parrots. Wherever possible, the palazzo's original features have been preserved, including an authentic fireplace in one of the rooms and magnificent ceiling frescoes in others.

The vibrant ambiance extends to the ground-floor restaurant, Il Magnifico, where elegant brass fittings harmonize with a backdrop of verdant foliage and animated portrayals of fauna. At the Butterfly Terrace, a rooftop bar, guests can savor cocktails while immersing themselves in breathtaking views of the city skyline before heading to the hotel's Lucie Gourmet restaurant, adorned with bold hues of peacock blue and pink.

Address: IL Tornabuoni Hotel, Via de' Tornabuoni, 3, 50123 Firenze FI, Italy

Price: Starting from £345 for double rooms

Georgia Tucker

Portrait Firenze
Best for: Ponte Vecchio views

Owned by the Ferragamo family, Portrait Firenze is an all-suite property that pays tribute to the 1950s and 1960s when Italian high fashion flourished, and Florence emerged as a magnet for celebrities. Black and white photos of movie stars grace the walls, with even a framed receipt for Marilyn Monroe's Ferragamo shoes on display. Floor-to-ceiling windows offer breathtaking vistas of the Arno River and the iconic Ponte Vecchio—don't forget to request a suite with a river-facing view.

At the ground-floor café, tables spill out onto the Lungarno, providing a front-row seat to observe life passing by. Alternatively, step onto the embankment and find yourself within easy reach of nearby attractions. The hotel also offers Vespa rentals, allowing guests to explore Florence and immerse themselves in a little dolce vita on two wheels.

Address: Portrait Firenze, Lungarno degli Acciaiuoli, 4, 50123 Firenze FI, Italy

Price: Starting from £510 for double rooms

Dario Garofalo
Best for: a sophisticated boutique

Upon ringing the doorbell, you gain entry to Dario Garofalo, a meticulously restored townhouse that invites guests to experience a truly refined Florentine retreat, as if visiting the home of a well-to-do friend. The Place, as it aspires to be, offers bespoke furnishings crafted by Florentine artisans and showcases local artworks throughout its communal spaces. Soft tones of green and cream echo the hues of the Santa Maria Novella façade, located just across the square.

The 20 elegantly designed rooms effortlessly blend sophistication and modern touches, boasting luxurious green and white marble bathrooms. The restaurant located on the ground floor offers an exquisite dining experience in an open-air setting, situated on a captivating square within the city. Here, guests can indulge in an array of culinary delights, including delectable offerings like Tuscan Calvana beef and meticulously crafted black Tortelli, generously filled with succulent prawns and zucchini. The culinary experience is complemented by stylish Richard Ginori china and an extensive selection of local Tuscan wines.

Address: The Place, Plaza di Santa Maria Novella, 7, 50123 Firenze FI, Italy

Price: Starting from £430 for double rooms

Ottantotto
Best for: affordable comforts

Nestled in the Oltrarno district, a short distance from Palazzo Pitti and the Boboli Gardens, Ottantotto is a delightful boutique hotel. Spanning four floors, its seven rooms tastefully combine classic and modern elements, featuring cotto floors, antique furnishings, and original architectural details. Room three boasts a headboard ingeniously integrated into a grand stone mantlepiece, accentuated by playful botanical and floral prints.

Georgia Tucker

The softly lit interiors and carefully placed books create an inviting atmosphere. A charming garden shaded by a centuries-old medlar tree and palm tree offers a tranquil setting for breakfast, served year-round (under a heated awning during winter). As the reception is only staffed until mid-afternoon, guests enjoy a sense of autonomy. An honesty bar is available in the lounge area, and during check-in, a personalized code is provided for access to the front door and a locker box containing the room key.

Address: Ottantotto Firenze, Via dei Serragli, 88, 50124 Firenze FI, Italy

Price: Starting from £140 for double rooms

Ad Astra
Best for: sophisticated, retro vibes

Situated in a serene location within the city walls, Ad Astra is a welcoming boutique hotel nestled in the expansive 17-acre private garden of Giardino Torrigiani. While the garden is not accessible to the public due to the residence of Marchese Torrigiani on the ground floor, guests can relish the view of the grounds from the charming terrace while enjoying a delightful breakfast brioche or savoring a glass of wine in the evening.

The proprietors have tastefully refurbished the hotel, incorporating a contemporary-retro design scheme that features intriguing curios, reclaimed furniture, and quirky vintage pieces sourced meticulously from flea markets across Europe. The lounge boasts a captivating 1960s optician's display cabinet, which serves as a bar counter, while the rooms are adorned with a myriad of knick-knacks and upcycled items, ranging from a retro cinema spotlight to a framed vintage Pucci scarf. Offering generous space, the rooms also boast claw-foot baths, adding a touch of decadence to the ambiance.

Address: Ad Astra, Via del Campuccio, 53, 50125 Firenze FI, Italy

Price: Starting from £120 for double rooms.

Four Seasons Hotel Firenze
Best for: Renaissance splendour

Occupying two grand Renaissance buildings, the opulent Four Seasons Hotel Firenze is nestled within the peaceful surroundings of the 11-acre Giardino della Gherardesca. This tranquil haven, adorned with centuries-old sequoias, maples, and conifers, offers interlacing paths, statues, and fountains. The interiors showcase exquisite artistic and cultural artifacts, with the 15th-century courtyard lobby featuring intricate stuccos and bar reliefs depicting classical and mythological events. The rooms are equally sumptuous, featuring luxurious fabrics, antique furnishings, and some even boasting vaulted ceilings and intricate frescoes.

The hotel prides itself on providing top-notch service, with a professional yet friendly staff who address guests by name. The facilities are among the finest in the city, including a delightful outdoor swimming pool, a luxurious spa, and ample amenities for children, such as a kids' club and playground. To enhance the overall experience, Michelin-starred dining is available at Il Palagio, offering a delightful garden setting during the summer months.

Georgia Tucker

Address: Four Seasons Hotel Firenze, Borgo Pinti, 99, 50121 Firenze FI, Italy

Price: Starting from £860 for double rooms.

Villa La Massa
Best for: peace and tranquillity

Imagining a wealthy Florentine family during the era of the Medicis seeking respite, Villa La Massa provides a serene riverside location, just a short distance from the bustling streets of Florence. As the sister property to the renowned Villa d'Este in Lake Como, this 13th-century villa is situated on the banks of the River Arno, surrounded by a 25-acre park adorned with olive, lemon, and cypress trees. The grounds offer a delightful swimming pool, a children's play area, and an appealing spa.

The rooms are spread across five buildings, each with its unique charm. Some exude a traditional Renaissance décor, featuring four-poster beds, tapestries, and elegant fabrics. Others showcase a contemporary aesthetic, with bespoke furnishings in earthy tones crafted by local artisans. In the evenings, the tranquil riverfront terrace of Il Verrocchio provides an idyllic setting to savor Mediterranean and Tuscan specialties while enjoying the soothing sound of the softly murmuring water.

Address: Villa La Massa, Via della Massa, 24, 50012 Candeli FI, Italy

Price: Starting from £445 for double rooms.

Hotel Lungarno
Best for: 20th-century art

Immaculately restored, this 16th-century residence houses a remarkable private art collection, featuring an original Picasso, a collection of Jean Cocteau, and over 450 other works predominantly by Italian artists. The hotel enjoys a superb riverfront location, with abundant natural light streaming through its expansive windows. The interiors exude a subtle nautical ambiance, with ivory fabrics, navy blue carpets, and dark wood fittings, evoking a sense of cruising along the Arno River.

The Picteau Bistrot and Bar, open throughout the day, offers a cozy living room atmosphere with captivating river views. For a Michelin-starred dining experience, the Borgo San Jacopo restaurant draws inspiration from 1950s glamour and offers a tiny terrace with magnificent views of the Ponte Vecchio.

Address: Hotel Lungarno, Borgo S. Jacopo, 14, 50125 Firenze FI, Italy

Price: Starting from £405 for double rooms.

Soprano Suites
Best for: vintage designs

Soprano Suites, situated within a 16th-century palazzo, exudes a charmingly unpretentious atmosphere, reminiscent of its sister-hotel Ad Astra. The property seamlessly blends whimsical vintage pieces and upcycled objects with original architectural elements, including ceiling frescoes and exposed beams. Noteworthy

Georgia Tucker

highlights include wooden seats salvaged from an old train, vintage typewriters, a table crafted from a water tank, and a curated selection of artworks adorning the walls.

The 13 generously sized rooms and suites feature lofty ceilings, some adorned with frescoes, creating an ambiance of spaciousness and grandeur. The cozy lounge area boasts an array of delightful market finds and shelves brimming with books, fostering a welcoming and laidback atmosphere. Guests are invited to linger, enjoying jazzy tunes, and indulging in all-day coffee and tea service.

Address: Soprano Suites, Via Maggio, 35, 50125 Firenze FI, Italy

Price: Starting from £105 for double rooms

Villa Cora
Best for: sumptuous interiors

Nestled in a serene residential area south of the city, away from the bustling crowds of central Florence, Villa Cora offers a tranquil retreat. This 19th-century villa showcases lavish interiors, seamlessly blending original period fittings such as splendid boiserie, glittering Murano chandeliers, and elaborate frescoes with a bold and contemporary selection of furnishings, including plush velvet plum armchairs and crystal glass tables.

The meticulously landscaped grounds feature lush rose bushes, creating a picturesque setting, and an inviting heated swimming pool shaded by majestic oak and yew trees. Guests can ascend to the rooftop terrace to immerse themselves in captivating city views or take advantage of the hotel's hillside location by strolling to Piazzale Michelangelo, one of Florence's most romantic viewpoints.

Address: Villa Cora, Viale Machiavelli, 18, 50125 Firenze FI, Italy

Price: Starting from £255 for double rooms

Helvetia & Bristol Firenze
Best for: centrality, wallpaper, pastries

Often, when a hotel is described as a "classic," a "grande dame," or a "beloved institution," it implies that the establishment is not merely old but also preserved in time. However, to become and remain a classic, a hotel must evolve. Such is the case with the Helvetia & Bristol, which has experienced its share of ups and downs since its opening in 1894. Nonetheless, under the ownership of the Starhotels group since 2016, the hotel has seen a surge of positive transformations.

The 64 existing rooms have been beautifully revitalized, adorned with swathes of silk and velvet, many of which are woven at the nearby Antico Setificio Fiorentino, an esteemed 18th-century textiles factory. In 2021, a new wing was introduced, situated in the former Florence headquarters of the Banca di Roma next door. The wing features 25 Anouska Hempel-designed rooms, each a poetic masterpiece in lustrous shades of grey.

The hotel also boasts LA SPA, the largest spa in the city center, which seamlessly combines authentic ancient elements, including real-life Roman ruins, with invigorating modern amenities such as the "Secret of Longevity" facial treatment. The hotel's fabulous bar, restaurant, and café, managed by the proprietors of Cibrèo in Sant'Angelo, offer exquisite dining experiences. Additionally,

Georgia Tucker

guests can relish the delectable pastries created by renowned pastry maker Iginio Massari, whose immaculate shop is conveniently located within the hotel. The breakfast experience in the ravishing Winter Garden is equally delightful, showcasing the fruits of Massari's labor.

One aspect of the Helvetia & Bristol that remains unchanged and timeless is its fantastic location opposite the Palazzo Strozzi, positioned between Via de' Tornabuoni and Piazza della Repubblica.

Address: Helvetia & Bristol Firenze – Starhotels Collezione, Via dei Pescioni, 2, 50123 Firenze FI, Italy

Price: Starting from approximately £400 (low season) and £700 (high season) for double rooms

Georgia Tucker

CHAPTER NINE

HEALTH AND SAFETY IN FLORENCE

Drink The Right Water
While tap water in Florence is safe for consumption, it is uncommon for locals to drink it. In trattorie and restaurants, you will be offered a choice of bottled mineral water, still or sparkling. Requesting tap water from a jug or carafe is discouraged.

Avoid Wandering Around Town Alone Late At Night
By exercising caution and using common sense, Florence can be a safe and comfortable city to explore. However, it is advisable to avoid the Santa Maria Novella area late at night when alone, as well as narrow and poorly lit alleys. Sticking to main thoroughfares that are well-illuminated is always a prudent choice.

Watch For Pickpockets
Crowded areas in Florence, particularly tourist hotspots like Piazza del Duomo, Ponte Vecchio, and San Lorenzo market, are attractive to pickpockets. It is essential to remain vigilant in these locations. Additionally, when traveling on crowded buses to

destinations like Piazzale del Michelangelo, Fiesole, and the airports, it is important to stay alert.

Buy Tickets Only From Official Ticket Offices And Websites

Outside the Uffizi and other locations in Florence, unauthorized sellers often advertise "skip the line" tickets. It is strongly advised not to purchase these tickets and instead rely on official museum channels for ticket purchases.

Don't Be Intimidated By Illegal Street Vendors – They're Only Human!

Florence has a presence of unauthorized street vendors offering counterfeit goods, such as selfie sticks, smartphone accessories, ponchos, and umbrellas. While generally harmless, it is sufficient to politely decline their offerings to deter them.

Georgia Tucker

MONEY SAVING TIPS

TIPS FOR SAVING MONEY ON TRANSPORTATION IN FLORENCE

Avoid Flying Into Florence Directly

When planning your trip to Florence, it is advisable to consider flying into nearby cities such as Rome, Pisa, or Milan instead of directly into Florence. Flight tickets to Florence tend to be more expensive compared to other Italian cities. By arriving in a neighboring city and then taking a train ride into Florence, not only can you avoid excessive jet lag but also have the opportunity to enjoy the scenic beauty of the Italian countryside.

Walk, Walk, And Walk!

The birthplace of the Renaissance, Florence, is best experienced by walking. The city's compact size allows you to traverse from one end to the other in just thirty minutes, granting ample time to leisurely explore and uncover the hidden gems that make Florence truly special. Stroll through the charming narrow streets, immerse yourself in the vibrant marketplace, marvel at the exquisite medieval architecture, and chance upon beautiful roadside churches adorned with frescoes.

Don't Hail Taxis, Call For Them!
In Florence, it is customary to call for taxi services rather than hailing them directly from the street. Taxis in Florence can be quite expensive, so it is wise to use them sparingly as a last resort. Many taxi companies often offer discounts and promotions, so it is advisable to check with the company in advance for any ongoing offers.

Get Your Bus Ticket Before Boarding!
While Florence is easily navigable on foot, utilizing the local bus network can save you valuable time. Remember to purchase bus tickets from authorized coffee shops or newsagents before boarding. Although tickets can also be acquired from the bus driver, they are subject to higher premium rates. Keep in mind that bus tickets in Florence remain valid for 90 minutes from the time of purchase.

TIPS FOR SAVING MONEY ON EATING IN FLORENCE

Florence's gastronomic delights reflect the city's rich artistic and architectural heritage.

Find Eateries Where Locals Abound
Avoid the tourist-laden restaurants in the city center and venture to areas away from the historical core to savor the most authentic Italian cuisine cherished by the locals. Consider engaging with the locals and seeking their recommendations for a genuine culinary

experience. Complement your meal with a delightful glass of wine to truly satisfy your taste buds.

Indulge In Streetside Food

When in the Tuscan capital, don't miss out on Florence's local specialties, including tripe, pizza, and lampredotto. These delectable dishes can be savored at small local establishments that primarily offer takeaway options. Enjoy your meal curbside or in one of Florence's charming parks for a memorable dining experience.

Have Your Coffee At The Bar!

In Florence, it is common to find bustling bars filled with patrons early in the day, as coffee shops are referred to as "bars" in the city. When indulging in coffee, head to the nearest bar and enjoy your beverage while standing at the counter. Sitting in the service area may incur additional charges. Italians often consume coffee while standing at the counter throughout the day, as table service can be significantly more expensive.

Buy Wine By The Bottles!

Florence, renowned for its Renaissance heritage, offers an array of exceptional wines at reasonable prices. A unique practice among locals is to visit wine shops or supermarkets with empty bottles and fill them directly from the tap, known as "Alla Spina." Embrace this local tradition and relish the abundance of high-quality red and white wines in Florence.

MORE TIPS TO SAVE MONEY IN FLORENCE

Be Smart In Selecting Areas For Accommodation

When visiting Florence with limited time, it is advisable to select a well-located hotel or dormitory within the city center. However, if you are seeking budget-friendly options, consider exploring residential areas outside the historic center. These areas, particularly on the opposite side of the Arno River, offer affordable accommodations while providing an authentic glimpse into the Florentine way of life.

Prep For Picnics!

Florence boasts numerous walled gardens adorned with captivating art installations. Take advantage of your spare time by leisurely strolling through these gardens and organizing a delightful picnic. Visit the San Lorenzo market to procure fresh produce like cheese and bread, and along the way, acquire wine or fresh fruit juices to enhance your outdoor dining experience.

Don't Miss Out On Free Attractions!

Florence offers a wealth of free attractions. Take a leisurely walk around the Santa Croce Basilica, admire the skilled craftsmanship of leather artists found throughout the city, or transport yourself back in time and admire the elegance of the Ponte Vecchio, the sole remaining medieval bridge in Florence. These experiences come at no cost and provide memorable encounters.

Georgia Tucker

Mondays Are Holidays For The Museum

As most museums in Florence are closed on Mondays, weekends tend to be crowded with visitors. To avoid the bustling weekend crowds, consider exploring alternative attractions in the nearby Piazza Della Signoria or take a peaceful stroll across the Ponte Vecchio Bridge.

Free Entry To State Museums

If your itinerary allows, schedule your visit to Florence on the first Sunday of any month between March and October. On these specific days, State Museums offer free admission, although it is important to note that the museums may be crowded. Noteworthy free attractions during this period include the Uffizi Garden, The Medici Chapels, Accademia Gallery, and The Pitti Palace.

Opt For Day Trips From Florence

If you find yourself with a few additional days in Florence, consider taking advantage of day trips to nearby destinations. By avoiding the need for new hotel accommodations, you can save a substantial amount of money while exploring new and exciting locations. Options include the charming Chianti region for an immersive wine-tasting experience, a visit to the iconic Leaning Tower of Pisa, or venturing to the awe-inspiring Cinque Terre, a UNESCO World Heritage site.

Maximize Online Bookings

Whether it pertains to airline or hotel reservations or purchasing entrance tickets to major attractions in Florence, utilizing online booking platforms can result in significant savings. Numerous cashback and discount vouchers are available online, allowing you to secure favorable rates and, in turn, save both money and valuable time that can be better spent relaxing instead of standing in long queues.

Georgia Tucker

CHAPTER TEN

GETTING AROUND FLORENCE

The best way to get around Florence is by foot. Walking is the most recommended way to navigate Florence. The city is relatively small, and it is possible to traverse it from one end to the other within approximately 30 minutes, passing by numerous recognizable landmarks. Alternatively, taking an ATAF bus is another viable option.

Transportation From Airports And Within The City

Many travelers arrive at Galileo Galilei Airport (PSA) in Pisa, making a stop at the Leaning Tower before taking a train to Florence's main station, Stazione di Firenze Santa Maria Novella. Another option is Amerigo Vespucci Airport (FLR) in Florence, from which buses or taxis can transport visitors to the city center. Renting a car is not advisable due to the city's narrow one-way streets and restricted pedestrian zones.

Exploring Florence On Foot

Florence is ideally suited for exploration on foot, except for individuals who prefer wearing heels. The city's ancient cobblestone streets can wear out high-heeled shoes quickly. It is recommended to wear comfortable walking shoes and discover the narrow streets, Renaissance architecture, charming shoe shops, and delectable Tuscan restaurants at a leisurely pace. While the streets are easy to navigate, those desiring guidance can consider joining a walking tour.

Bus

If walking becomes tiring, efficient ATAF buses are available in Florence. Remember to validate your ticket upon boarding. One-way tickets can be purchased for approximately 1.50 euros ($1.70) at local Italian convenience stores.

For those who prefer not to rely on walking or need to reach areas outside the center, buses provide extensive coverage across all neighborhoods of the city. Additionally, bus services connect Florence to the neighboring village of Fiesole (Line 7) and other surrounding communities. Bus operations generally run until approximately 11:00 pm, although specific schedules may vary by route.

Car

Cars and Florence are not an ideal combination. The city center restricts access to tourist drivers, as designated areas marked with "ZTL" (Limited Traffic Zone) are exclusively for authorized vehicles. Furthermore, numerous pedestrian zones and narrow one-way streets make driving a challenging experience. Special permits are required for driving within the restricted zones. If necessary, it is recommended to park cars on the city outskirts in designated parking facilities and either walk or take a taxi into the city.

Georgia Tucker

Navigating Florence by car can be challenging due to traffic congestion, the unique road layout of the historic center, and limited public parking options. Additionally, entering the Limited Traffic Zone (LTZ) without the necessary permit can result in substantial fines. However, should travelers choose to drive their vehicles or rent one, it is advisable to select a hotel in Florence with parking facilities or utilize private parking services. In either case, temporary LTZ permits will be provided for accessing the city center.

Taxi

Taxis can be quite expensive in Florence, with fares starting at approximately 3 euros ($3.40) on weekdays and Saturdays, and higher rates on Sundays and between 10 p.m. and 6 a.m. Travelers on a budget should use taxis sparingly, often relying on them solely for transportation to and from Florence Train Station (Stazione di Firenze Santa Maria Novella). It is important to note that hailing taxis are illegal, and it is advisable to call ahead or visit official taxi ranks located at major squares.

Florence boasts a considerable number of taxis, identifiable by their white color. However, during Saturday nights and significant events, availability may be limited. It is worth noting that taxi fares tend to be relatively high, with a short journey within the center costing between 10 and 20 euros, depending on factors such as luggage, public holidays, or nighttime rates.

Taxis can be hailed on the street or contacted via phone (reservations are not accepted). An alternative is to use the IT

TAXI app to request a cab. Two taxi companies operate in Florence, reachable at the following phone numbers:

+39 055 4390

+39 055 4242

Taxi stands are conveniently located in prominent squares such as Piazza della Stazione, Piazza Santa Maria Novella, and Piazza Santa Croce.

Public Transportation In Florence

The public transportation system in Florence primarily serves as a means of accessing and departing from the historic center, which is conveniently walkable in size. Although buses often experience overcrowding and delays, the tram network offers more reliable service.

A single ticket, valid for both buses and trams, can be purchased for 1.50 euros at tobacco shops or through vending machines located in Piazza San Marco and at tram stations. Alternatively, travelers can conveniently obtain tickets using the TABNET mobile app.

By Tram

The tram network currently consists of two functioning lines:

T1 connects Santa Maria Novella station to the suburb of Scandicci.

T2 connects Santa Maria Novella train station to Peretola Airport.

Additional tram lines are currently under construction. Trams operate until 2:00 am, offering extended service hours.

By Bike

Cycling is a delightful and cost-effective mode of transportation in Florence, particularly during the warmer months. Bicycles can be rented for a nominal fee, with some rental services even offering electric bikes. Another convenient option is the MoBike bike-sharing service, which allows registered users to unlock available bicycles using a dedicated app.

Although the city features some dedicated bike lanes, their availability is limited, primarily encircling the center and connecting it to the outskirts. During crowded periods in the historic center, maneuvering on a bicycle may prove challenging, necessitating dismounting until the crowd disperses.

Bike And E-Bike Sharing

Florence offers a bike-sharing program operated by Mobike, featuring both regular and electric bicycles. While regular bicycles are sturdy but heavy, electric ones provide a more enjoyable experience, particularly during summer. To access the shared bikes, users must download the Mobike app, connect their credit cards, and adhere to designated parking areas to avoid additional charges.

Shared E-Scooters

In addition to bike sharing, Florence now offers electric shared scooters provided by three companies: TiMove, Bit Mobility, and

Bird. Similar to bike sharing, users must download the corresponding app, link their credit cards, and consult the app's map to locate available scooters.

HOW TO MAKE THE MOST OUT OF YOUR TRIP TO FLORENCE

Florence, Italy offers a wealth of attractions and activities that can make planning your trip overwhelming. However, embracing the essence of this captivating city is key – take strolls through its streets, immerse yourself in the piazzas' ambiance, and relish the exquisite cuisine and wines. Nevertheless, if you desire to make the most of your visit and ensure a fulfilling experience, here are some expert tips to guide you.

City Tours

Embark on a guided city tour to orient yourself and gain a comprehensive overview of the city's major highlights. These tours, led by knowledgeable guides, offer intriguing insights into Florence's history, culture, and art. Among the highly recommended tours is the Segway tour, enabling you to effortlessly explore the city on an electric scooter while marveling at its sights. Additionally, various companies offer walking tours, bike tours, and delectable food tours, allowing you to savor the local cuisine.

Georgia Tucker

2. Visit The Museums
Florence boasts world-renowned art museums, including the Uffizi Gallery and the Accademia Gallery. Housing an extraordinary collection of Renaissance masterpieces by artists such as Botticelli, Michelangelo, and Leonardo da Vinci, these museums provide a captivating glimpse into the city's history and culture. Even if art isn't your primary interest, visiting these museums is highly recommended. For those with limited time, guided museum tours offered by reputable companies can optimize your visit.

3. Climb To The Top Of The Duomo
The Duomo, a magnificent cathedral situated in the heart of Florence, stands as an iconic landmark. Its awe-inspiring interior and exterior, adorned with intricate sculptures and stained glass windows, deserve exploration. The highlight, however, lies in ascending to the top of the dome, offering breathtaking panoramic views of Florence and its picturesque surroundings. Bravery may even lead you to venture onto the cathedral's roof, an experience not to be missed – just ensure a firm grip!

4. Shop Till You Drop
Florence presents a paradise for shoppers, with an array of shops and markets catering to diverse tastes, from designer fashion to handmade leather goods. For an authentic Italian shopping experience, venture into the city's open-air markets, where bargaining for souvenirs, clothing, and more is part of the charm. Caution is advised, as hours and funds may quickly disappear while perusing the enticing stalls. Additionally, Florence's streets

are lined with high-end boutiques, making it effortless to find that coveted designer piece.

5. Sample The Local Cuisine

Sampling the local cuisine is one of the greatest pleasures of travel, and Florence does not disappoint in this regard. From fresh pasta and pizza to hearty stews and delightful desserts, there is an abundance of flavors to relish. Be sure to treat yourself to the city's renowned gelato – an unforgettable experience. Furthermore, no visit to Florence would be complete without savoring a glass or two of Chianti, the iconic red wine of the region. For an immersive culinary adventure, consider participating in cooking classes offered by local restaurants, allowing you to learn about the cuisine and take home cherished recipes.

6. Relax In The Parks

Amidst the sightseeing and shopping, find respite in one of Florence's many parks. The Boboli Gardens and the Giardino Bardini are popular choices, offering serene landscapes, captivating sculptures, and picturesque vistas of the city. During the summer, cool off in one of the city's outdoor pools to escape the heat. Moreover, the city's parks and gardens provide excellent opportunities for people-watching and immersing themselves in the local atmosphere.

Georgia Tucker

CONCLUSION

Congratulations on discovering the beautiful city of Florence, Italy! We hope that this travel guide has provided you with all the information you need to plan an unforgettable trip to this incredible destination.

As we've shown throughout this guide, it's possible to experience the wonders of Florence without breaking the bank. From free museums and galleries to budget-friendly food options and walking tours, there are plenty of ways to explore the city without overspending.

So, what are you waiting for? Put on your walking shoes and immerse yourself in the rich history and culture of Florence. Discover the incredible art, architecture, and cuisine that make this city one of the most beloved destinations in the world.

As you explore Florence, remember to take advantage of all the city has to offer. Visit iconic landmarks like the Duomo and Ponte Vecchio, explore the winding streets of the historic center, and savor the flavors of traditional Tuscan cuisine.

By following the tips and advice in this guide, you can make the most of your time in Florence while still staying within your budget. Whether you're a seasoned traveler or a first-time visitor, we're confident that Florence will capture your heart and leave you with memories that will last a lifetime.

Thank you for choosing " Florence Travel Guide 2023-2024: How to Spend a Day in Florence Without Breaking the Bank and Walk and Explore the Historic Center in Italy!" as your travel guide. We wish you safe travels and unforgettable experiences in this beautiful city. PLEASE LEAVE A REVIEW OR RATING AFTER READING OUR GUIDE!!!!

Georgia Tucker

Printed in Great Britain
by Amazon